FROM THE TOP

The Real Secrets of Business Success

FROM THE TOP

ISBN-13: 978-1484859155
ISBN-10: 1484859154

Produced by:

Fairfax Media
2 Hereford St
Freeman's Bay
Auckland
New Zealand

All photographs courtesy of Fairfax Media.
Except:
Front and back cover art courtesy of iStock
Ted Lees from 1940s supplied by Ted Lees. Sir Richard Carter supplied by Carter Holt Harvey. Sir John Ilott portrait and Edmonds book and produce supplied. Graeme Lowe historic photo supplied by Lowe Corporation. Marianne Caughey Smith Preston portrait supplied. George Beca portrait supplied. Sir John Plimmer portrait supplied. Izzi Morris supplied the photo of her team. Sir James Fletcher Snr portrait supplied. Sir John Logan Campbell supplied.

Preface

ACKNOWLEDGEMENT

Business Hall of Fame laureates

This book could not have been produced without the gracious commitment of the time and thoughts of the businessmen and women who agreed to be interviewed. They not only made time in their busy schedules, they also often revealed startlingly personal insights into their lives and what drove them to success. They are all laureates of the Fairfax Media New Zealand Business Hall of Fame. Established in 1994 by the Young Enterprise Trust, the Business Hall of Fame now has more than 100 members, individuals who, through enterprise, have helped build the economic prosperity and social development of this country.

Young Enterprise Trust

Tribute is also due to the great work of the Young Enterprise Trust, whose foresight saw the launch of the Business Hall of Fame. The charitable trust's vision is to grow a more prosperous New Zealand through enterprise by helping educate and transform students – giving a platform for our future business leaders to grow.

Creating an enterprising spirit in young people is needed, regardless of whether they are going to set up their own company or work for someone else, whether their organisation is large or small, whether the business is a commercial business, government agency or not for profit organisation. Being enterprising is more than the process of starting a business. It is about identifying, valuing and capturing opportunities. It is about taking ownership, exercising initiative and showing leadership.

At the core of being enterprising is the ability to understand the financial situation and wider economy and to spot opportunities as they arise. YES is dedicated to embedding financial literacy in our young people – an aim which Fairfax Media fully endorses and pursues through its own business publications.

Fairfax Media

Thanks also is due to the work of the journalists of Fairfax Media, particularly those of the business team, many of who carried out interviews and produced stories which contributed to this work. Thanks also to business journalist, the late Graeme Hunt, who died in 2010 and was for many years the driving force behind the Business Hall of Fame.

CONTENTS

FROM THE TOP

The Real Secrets of Business Success

Edited by David Gadd

Introduction

THE LESSONS OF LIFE

Between them they have shaped this country, forged its economy, provided jobs and livelihoods to thousands, become household names and in some cases defined the very way we see ourselves as New Zealanders. They are our greatest business leaders – laureates of the Fairfax Media Business Hall of Fame.

They number more than 100, spanning the history of business in New Zealand from pioneer days to the present. They lived through boom times, recession and depression. Some built mighty industrial empires from nothing, then lost it all; others passed on businesses through the family, each generation building and enlarging. Some through their vision and energy created entire industries that powered the nation forward; others through the same driven desire for change, destroyed industries through disruptive innovation.

The life stories of each are filled with lessons of the real, practical experience of running a business - identifying opportunities, making decisions, confronting and overcoming problems, motivating, harnessing, organising, creating teams, companies, cultures and wealth.

Once you talk to these business greats and trace their personal stories, some common threads emerge. These threads are the basis of this work you are about to read, based on the hallmarks of what makes a great business leader. These traits include a restless energy, vision and strategic foresight, courageous risk taking, humility and an enormous generosity of reinvesting back into the community.

The Business Hall of Fame is a resource of immense value to anyone with aspirations to themselves forge a career in the world of business and enterprise. Laureates have given unprecedented access to Fairfax Media in the writing of this work, reflecting on their careers and sharing their insights. This is a priceless collective wisdom available nowhere else. They are the hard lessons learnt by the country's top business men and women as they worked their way to the top. It was seldom an easy journey.

These are the real secrets of business success.

Chapter One

BUSINESS ACHIEVERS REVEAL THE REAL SECRETS OF SUCCESS

He was blown up by a mine in the North African desert, fired on by fighter planes, fended floating bombs off bridges during the advance into Europe and was a founding member of the country's SAS unit.

For Ted Lees the maelstrom of war was his training ground rather than university and textbooks.

It all began with what is probably still a fairly typical conversation held in many a home. A family friend threw a critical eye over 14-year-old Lees, asking his father "What are you going to do with him."

The reply: "He's rebelling and I want to teach him to do as he's told."

The plan was for young Ted to train as an accountant. But he had other ideas, wanting to be an engineer. So he quit school at 14, taking himself into a hands-on apprenticeship. Then as soon as World War II broke out two years later, he enlisted aged just 16.

The army got his considerable and instinctive engineering skills. It also got that rebellious streak. "I got into trouble everywhere I went for doing things too soon," he said.

But it was an attitude that was invaluable, to him and to the men who came to depend on him

"Here was I with some of these things I had never seen before, thrown in the deep end," he said. "It was a case of doing it."

Ted Lees' name may not be familiar to most people. He's not one of the rock stars of New Zealand business, nor a household name. Part of our largely ignored business heritage, Lees is, nonetheless, one of our business greats. With no formal tertiary qualifications and barely any secondary education, he built an industrial company that produced the machines which powered our primary industries – from farming to forestry to construction – through the hey days of the 1950s to 1970s. It allowed the container freight revolution to take off, making the growth

3

of those decades a practical reality and ushering in the modern New Zealand economy.

You could make the mistake of writing him off as a dinosaur from another era, with no relevance to today's management challenges. But in fact he is, in many ways, the epitome of everything modern management is about. This is because his company, Lees Industries, was intensely focused on sectors at a time when they were undergoing immense and rapid transformation. It would be hard to find a better individual example than this gritty, determined man of learning in the real world, the clichéd school of hard knocks. Wherever he went he eagerly soaked up new experiences and skills. Later when opportunity arose, he applied them in fresh, startling ways to achieve breakthroughs. But even more importantly, he knew his company depended on embracing the change confronting it and driving solutions for clients. To do this required innovation embedded at every level of the company. Lees describes himself as "a bad student, but a good teacher." He was passionate about ensuring everyone at every level could contribute to solutions.

In the early 1990s Peter Senge popularised the concept of the Learning Organisation though his book The Fifth Discipline. It was seen as the latest management theory that best described the way in which firms of the 21st century will need to structure themselves to meet the challenges of an increasingly dynamic world. It basically argues that old models of centralised command and control are no longer appropriate for companies which need to be far more responsive, nimble, and flexible. Instead, Senge said learning and decision-making needs to be driven through every aspect of an organisation, to the coal face. That is, the Lees model. The Learning Organisation is proposed as the best response to a period of significant change. Lees instinctively adopted a similar structure when he faced a specific business environment of significant change.

Even when interviewed at age 87, Lees had a restless spirit and inventive mind. Critically he managed to meld that with an entrepreneurial appetite for risk-taking and the discipline of a hard headed businessman to build and run a multi-million dollar turnover business. The management lessons he accrued through hard graft are interesting to consider. He was a believer in strong leadership from the front, not necessarily in an old- fashioned autocratic manner, but in terms of demonstrating and personifying his business' values. He knew the virtues of sound organisational set up, the understanding that a business must be structured and focused in the way it pursues growth and attainment of its goals. But equally, he prized innovation. It was the springboard of his business and he was careful to retain that as his company grew.

Lastly, he knew the value of relationships with customers, suppliers and staff. If you examine Lees' lessons from a more theoretical perspective, they demonstrate the basic tenets of good management.

Trying to define business leadership, to reduce it into a meaningfully, understandable sequence which can be studied and learned, involves consideration of managerial functions, skills, activities, roles and personality types and leadership styles - the entire panoply of managerial dexterity. Many consider it a quixotic task. But essentially what a leader does is to give direction to the company, a division or team, by identifying opportunities, setting goals to exploit such opportunities, co-coordinating the best use of resources and leading people to achieve those goals. This normally involves focusing on the customer, being dedicated to making the best products, and providing the best value service in the right place. Results must be monitored and adjustments made to ensure the goals are being achieved in the most efficient and effective way possible given the limitations of the company and vagaries of the business environment.

In short during any given day a business leader has to think and plan, has to lead and deal with people, has to organise, control, make decisions and has to simply *do*. And this is what Lee's talks about when he reflects on the key drivers behind how he built and ran his business. He is talking about planning, organising, controlling, leading.

THE UNIVERSAL LAWS OF BUSINESS

It is testament to the universality of basic principles of business leadership that the Lees philosophy of building a strong, effective company which was gained through personal experience, lie at the heart of most successful business ventures. Many of New Zealand's top business people identify similar key issues, challenges and solutions. What is revealed is that there is a science of management that textbooks and theoreticians seek to distil, and then there is the art of management, the ephemeral genius of the master practitioners which often defies attempts to dissect it. One of the theoreticians who has endeavoured to summarise successful executive traits is former Harvard and Stanford professor Robert L Katz. He made this critical point:

"… this quest for the executive stereotype has become so intense that many companies, in concentrating on certain specific traits or qualities, stand in danger of losing sight of their real concern: *what a man can accomplish*."

This is why Lees and his ilk are important. They have accomplished. Their accomplishments can be weighted, determined, valued in dollar terms. They are judged on the change they made in industry practice, in the political and governance impact that flowed in the wake of their achievements, on the imprint they left on the economy and the country's development. It is insights gained from men and women of accomplishment that you will find here - looking at the top 100 plus leaders from New Zealand's business history spanning back to the 1840s, the laureates of the Fairfax Media New Zealand Business Hall of Fame. We offer you here an unparalleled view of the thinking of our most successful business brains and how they built successful businesses. It provides examples you can sift through, consider and usefully integrate to improve your own business skills no matter where you sit in your career.

Katz usefully categorised the skills of managers into three broad groupings – technical, conceptual and human. It is those latter two we will concentrate on. Management can involve a multitude of individual technical skills depending on your industry and it is an important element, often forming part of the 'expert power' which is part of the basis of leadership. But at top levels within business it is more often a hygiene factor. The ability to directly carry out a technical task becomes increasingly less important the higher you rise and instead a leader concentrates on depending upon others to complete tasks, as Katz found in his research. A leader instead devotes time to thinking through issues. It is the conceptual and the human skills which become transportable skills across any industry in the top tier of executive management.

Strong managerial and leadership skills are increasingly important to all managers in companies in every sector. Today's companies must remain competitive in the face of a tough environment – the turbulence of the 2008/09 global financial crisis which brought with it changes in the allocation of capital, hiring and resourcing of companies will last for some time. There is the ongoing and inescapable paradigm shift of economic power from the USA to China – from the developed countries to emerging powerhouses and a subsequent impact on trade and finance. The ongoing pace of technological change affects business models, tools and organisational structure. There are the inevitable generational changes of the work force and consumers. In New Zealand where we have traditionally lacked skilled white collar workers, we are particularly dependent on migration. This often accelerates secondary issues such as housing bubbles and social shifts in consumer demand. All of this feeds into the cyclical trends in the wider economy and in particular sectors but also often leads to disruption which can permanently change market structures. Through all of this, successful business leaders must hold a clear vision of where they are going and how they will get there, engaging employees, consistently appealing to

Lifelong Learning

Learning never stops for the best leaders. It is a lifelong process. Sir Stephen Tindall stood in a classroom of Clover Park Middle School in Otara, giving just that advice to a rapt audience. "Up to year 11, I struggled at school. I had two years at year 11." But that did not hold him back, and indeed he embraced learning outside of school, often taking on board more valuable lessons than taught in the classroom. "All my life I have continued to learn. Learning never stops." And looking around at the teenagers before him, he commented that the learning those students would encounter through their lives after school and how they applied it would have a marked impact on this country's development. "In another 20 years the world will be very different. This is really the epicentre of New Zealand. The challenge to you is to take New Zealand forward."

consumers, doing more with less and coping with the one constant of life – change. A strong leader must recognise the challenges, take the appropriate approach to respond and drive a company to sustainable success.

This highlights the strengths of examining the careers of the Business Hall of Fame laureates, in that they span the history of business in New Zealand and provide often real life examples of most of the challenges businesses face. Indeed, you will find that these entrepreneurs were often disruptive forces themselves. They embraced change. They are role models for coping with change and bringing an enlightened view to organising companies, harnessing and motivating human capital, focusing on customers and inclusive decision making. Eyeing opportunity, taking risks, problem solving and forging strong, adaptive cultures were the hallmarks of our top business people.

The vital statistics of New Zealand's business environment are worth noting and reflecting upon as they highlight the constancy of challenge and change in our business environment. There are approximately 470,000 businesses in New Zealand at any given time employing, or rather providing a living for and sustaining the families of, around 2.1 million Kiwis. Of that number just 0.5 percent, or around 2,500 companies employ more than 100 staff, and around 47 percent of all workers have their jobs in those firms. In other words, we have a small pool of blue chip companies in which to climb the corporate ladder. Those businesses are split mainly between Auckland – around 1000 – and Wellington and Canterbury with around 350 a piece.

Of the rest of the companies of New Zealand, 97 percent are small, employing fewer than 20 staff and if we narrow to an even more specific subset, 68 per cent are sole trading owner operators with no staff.

And it is from this group that we must hope the new big corporates of the future will emerge, if our economy is to grow. The task of leading your own business with no or few staff is no less daunting than being CEO of an NZX top 50 corporate.

Each year around 50,000 people with hope in their heart and dreams of financial independence launch businesses. On average 8,000 of them will have gone under within a year and within seven years, 30,000 or two thirds will have disappeared. The lessons of those who have gone before, who have climbed from no employees to corporate giants, is therefore as salient to the small business operator as to those planning careers in CBD towers. And amongst the Business Hall of Fame laureates are those who have grown companies from no staff to thousands.

HUGH PERRETT: Shopping for the right strategy

He retired far too young – he still had another five years in him.

What greater compliment could there be for a business leader, than colleagues and your own board, lamenting the fact you've opted to chase the rewards of retirement instead of staying behind the desk.

Hugh Perrett, former managing director of FoodStuffs NZ, the giant supermarket co-operative which runs the New World and Pak'N Save chains in New Zealand, still attracts such accolades after stepping down in 2001.

His leadership is recognised by Foodstuffs store owners as having transformed the business from industry laggard to dominant player. It is also a prime illustration of leadership principals put into practical operation in a pressure cooker test of skill and will. When Perrett joined Foodstuffs in 1977, starting out as general manager of the Auckland region, the business was facing serious problems.

"We really were the rear runner if you like in the supermarket business. I wouldn't say we were in danger of going under or anything like that but certainly we weren't making the grade," he says.

It was then Perrett revealed himself as an almost text book model of a transformational leader. Big Hairy Audacious Goal, the BHAG, is a management buzz word coined in the 1990s, but before the phrase was developed, Perrett exemplified what it means. Faced with being behind the pack, his reaction?

"The big challenge was not how do we catch them up but how do we pass them and how do we become the dominant player the market place."

And that they did.

Under Perrett's guidance Foodstuffs' national turnover grew from $1.1 billion to $4.8 billion while it's national share of supermarket business rose from 12 per cent to 55 per cent, and the national share of wholesale grocery business to more than 60 per cent.

It became New Zealand's second-largest business and was recognised as a world class model for independent grocers and wholesalers. Behind those startling statistics were highlights the former grocery boss still savours.

He led the development of Foodstuffs' private label ranges such as Pam's, Budget and Fresh Express which grew to contribute more than $400 million to retail group turnover. He also introduced beer and wine to supermarkets, in the face of initial opposition from the breweries. He worked closely with then Shell New Zealand chief executive Charles Harrison to introduce the Fly Buys loyalty scheme. He was responsible for the development of Gilmours into New Zealand's leading cash-and-carry wholesaling operation.

And of course there is the launch of Pak'N Save, which Perrett rightly and proudly sees as his greatest legacy in terms of impact on the country.

He says Pak'N Save's introduction was pivotal in driving pricing down in New Zealand and still maintains that role today.

"No doubt the opposition pricing has been pulled down by Pak'N Save.

So I think it isn't idle to say that Pak'N Save on a permanent ongoing basis has meant up to 15 per cent savings to the New Zealand public."

If you ask him to look back on the legacy he left for the business itself, that classic and structured leadership mind shows through.

He ticks off a veritable Pak'N Save shopping list of a strategy map, a balanced scorecard, call it what you will – it's a blueprint of business building factors every leader should deliver on and which every up and coming manager can learn from.

In financial asset management he revised Foodstuffs' constitutional documents to protect the group against predatory attack and left behind a major land banking strategy because few issues are as important to supermarkets as location.

From an operational process and innovation perspective he embedded a comprehensive understanding of key retail format principles and a competitive mixed distribution system.

In product lines the private label strategy has been a clear competitive advantage.

And in people management he established a robust recruitment process to identify future owner operators of the grocery stores.

Of course Perrett is quick to give credit to others, saying such achievements were the result of a talented management team, particularly in property acquisition, store design and consumer marketing. But undeniably underpinning the Foodstuff success was getting the strategy right. And that is fairly and squarely due to Perrett.

This is a man who understood the nature of leadership and about the structure of organisational strength. Put on the spot, Perrett sums it up thus: "The leader must provide clarity of purpose and vision."

Arguably his greatest accomplishment, given that he came into a business that was drifting at the back of the industry, was quietly achieved without the fanfare of new product launches or store openings. It happened at his desk in 1979.

He wrote a mission statement, an articulation of core values and operating philosophy. "It provided a strong, ongoing point of focus for the company," he says. And it still forms the guiding principles for the business.

So if we cut down to the core of it all, what is the Perrett secret to business? Differentiating from competitors and identifying with consumers. Basic. No frills. A Pak'N Save of a management concept.

The skill of course is in execution, the tough task of keeping that approach at the forefront, taking it from high-minded concept and transforming it into everyday application and ensuring each tactical decision they took aligned to that strategic goal.

Perrett, through a mixture of hands-on management and strategic thinking, excelled in executing his plan. Perhaps the grocery business was simply the business environment he was born to be in. You could say it was in his blood. When he took the helm at Foodstuffs he was following his father's footsteps – Harry Perrett was general manager of Wellington Foodstuffs from 1937 to 1953.

"If anyone inspired me, it was my father," he says.

From the age of four he and twin Malcolm, were running around the warehouse in Wellington and the business was part of family life. He is imbued with institutional knowledge, an encyclopaedic understanding of the development of the grocery business.

In addition to his Foodstuffs work, Perrett was a non-executive director of New Zealand Dairy Foods from 2001 to 2005 and a non-executive director of Goodman Fielder.

His pro bono work includes non-executive directorships with Business Mentors NZ, the Christian Healthcare Trust and AUT Enterprises. He was also an invited lecturer at the University of Auckland's business incubator, Icehouse.

+ Sources for this profile were a one to one interview by David Gadd with Hugh Perrett and interviews with former colleagues.

GRAEME LOWE: Disruptive force of nature

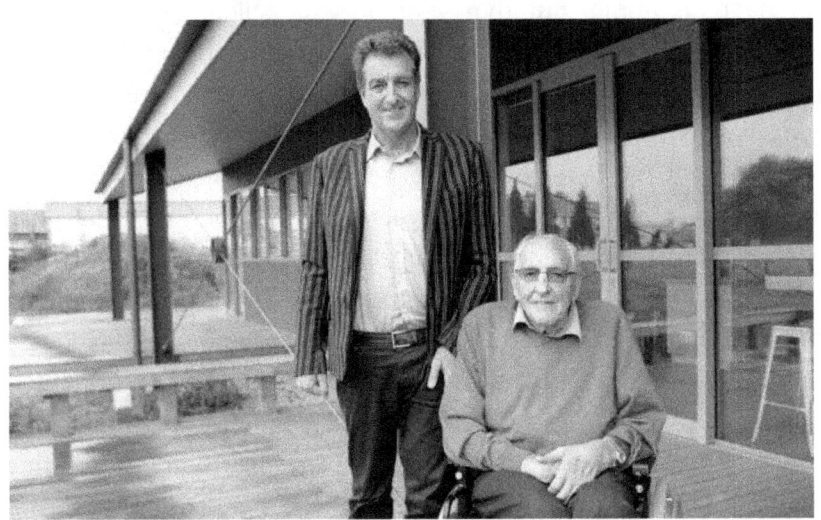

The late Graeme Lowe was built like Goliath but played the role of David. Two-metres tall, dashing, but down-to-earth, he made an indelible impression on New Zealand.

He has gone down in history as the man who revolutionised this country's meat industry. From an early age his 'just do it' attitude, ambition and vision were evident and he was always going to be one of those disruptive forces that shake up complacent industries. To family, friends and colleagues he was a self-made man, single-minded and headstrong, but led by his heart.

Graeme Eric Selby Lowe was born in Newcastle, England, to New Zealand mother Joan and English businessman Eric, who died when his son was just 11. The young Graeme, one of three boys, developed a love of the sea and would spend full days on fishing boats from the age of six. He was sporty and though not particularly interested in schoolwork, still made his mark. A housemaster at his school wrote: "It would hardly be possible to imagine a boy more thoughtful or helpful or more deserving of the goodwill of everyone in the house."

The lanky Lowe left school aged 18 in 1952 to join a local tannery, one of four near his home. But that year he was called up for national service and joined the Royal Navy, reaching the rank of sub-lieutenant before returning to the tannery. His leadership skills came to the fore again in sport. Lowe took on the role of club captain at the Hull and East Riding rugby club and reversed its poor form to help make it one of the best sides in the north of England. He was just 21.

Although his mother and her new husband then emigrated to New Zealand, Lowe remained in Britain, wanting to see out the end of the 1957 rugby season. During a match in London, a team- mate showed him a newspaper advert. "Master mariner having twice completed similar voyage seeks enthusiasts to crew well-found motor yacht to New Zealand via Jamaica, Panama and Tahiti. Leaving March." Wanting adventure rather than just a passage on a liner, Lowe gave it a shot

Against more than 800 applicants for 10 crew positions, Lowe won a berth. But it proved to be more adventure than he anticipated. The Summer Rose, a 21-metre, sail-assisted fishing boat with a 160hp diesel motor was not initially seaworthy and its skipper was known to like a drink or two. After the boat arrived in port in Jamaica the skipper sailed away without the crew. Lowe got his gear back after a chase but had to find another way to New Zealand - via a ship bound for Australia from Panama.

Of the ten who set sail for New Zealand only Lowe and one other made it. There is an early photo of him on Summer Rose, standing with arms crossed beneath the boom, towering over his shipmates. He has the unmistakable bearing and profile of a leader.

It was a trait he kept throughout his life, said his son, Andy, and never more so than in his final two decades when afflicted by Parkinson's Disease.

"I think what drove him was a love of people. He didn't care about status, race, religion, age, what school you went to . . . People related to that and it meant they were willing to follow him.

SUMMER ROSE

"The thing that inspires me is that in health anyone can be heroic and brave and a mentor and live by their principles. It's in sickness that you see real strength. Here's a man who was once in control of so much but now struggled to lift a glass of water to his mouth, yet he never complained."

Graeme Lowe died in 2012, aged 77, just two weeks after being inducted into the Business Hall of Fame. His story is one of all the classic traits of an entrepreneur determined to make his mark.

Shortly after landing in New Zealand, Lowe found work as an assistant production manager at Birdseye Foods Ltd's Christchurch plant. His zest for innovation and his penchant for lateral thinking became a hallmark of his time with the company, but not always with the best results.

In a misplaced bid to improve the yield of chickens going through a mincer he once instructed staff to crank it up to maximum speed and put whole carcasses through, bones and all. Yield improved dramatically, but he was soon confronted by an apoplectic factory boss demanding answers.

Lowe was barred from the factory, given the keys of a Morris Minor and dispatched to become a travelling buyer of meat, fish and poultry.

His charm and sense of humour meant it was a job in which he excelled, and later led to his being moved to Hawke's Bay, where he became company buyer for Unilever (Birdseye's owner).

Meanwhile he had fallen in love with Wellingtonian Jenny Allen, who he married in 1960 and the timing was right for another entrepreneurial trait to emerge - shaping your own destiny.

By 1964, at the age of 29, Lowe began looking for other opportunities. He borrowed a deposit from his father-in-law and roped in a few friends to buy a wholesale and retail butcher's plant in Hastings called Dawn Meats. The vendor, Cedric Jones, reckoned Lowe would go bust and he would be able to buy the business back for a bargain in six months.

But characteristically Lowe put his head down. He started at 4am working alongside the butchers and usually worked into the night. It was he who drove the company's Commer van to the Tomoana meatworks to collect the livestock, loading as many as he could onto the van, often tying some to the roof. He was a dynamic new force in an industry accustomed to a staid and unquestioning regularity. The established "old boys" did not take kindly to this upstart.

Soon, Lowe saw the future was in exporting. But the late 1960s were the days of heavy regulation. He had inherited a couple of packhouse licences from Dawn Meats that allowed him to pack a limited number of cattle. But only export-licensed slaughter and processing plants could kill the stock for export. Until he had one of these he would always be at the mercy of the big boys and the Meat Board, which ruled who could have licences.

What followed was a lengthy battle that saw Lowe take on the establishment and finally win the right to conduct business free of stifling regulation. Along the way Lowe, frustrated at constraints forced on him by Hawke's Bay meat companies, bought an old pork meatworks in Hawera, T H Walker and Sons, that held a slaughter licence. The plant was upgraded for beef and put into full throttle.

By the mid 1980s Dawn Meats was exporting about 2200 tonnes of chilled beef a year. It had been granted a licence to slaughter in Hawke's

Bay as long as it combined with competitor Richmonds. They formed Pacific Meats and in November 1981, Pacific's Oringi plant near Dannevirke was opened by the then Prime Minister Rob Muldoon.

A combination of economic factors, an end of subsidies and a drop in livestock numbers in the late 80s resulted in Lowe making the reluctant decision to sell out of Dawn Meats and Pacific. He started a new venture, Lowe Walker, and added further plants in Te Aroha, Dargaville, Paeroa and Hastings. Between 1988 and 1991 the company's turnover rose from $35 million to $225m.

In 1998 Lowe sold the plants to Richmond and formed Lowe Corporation, which specialised in by-products, with rendering and tannery plants in Hawera, Hastings, Te Aroha, Auckland, Tuakau and Christchurch. Now in the hands of Andy Lowe, it is New Zealand's largest privately owned independent hide, skin, protein recycling, processing and exporting company and also has interests in other agri-business companies and property.

"When I was about 7 years old, all Graeme did was work so if we wanted to see him we had to go with him," Andy said. "Back then it was just a little butcher shop with one office in the front. Graeme would be in there and I'd be out the back making a nuisance with the sausage makers or hounding him for some money to go down the road to buy a pie."

Another essential characteristic of entrepreneurs is their ability to recognise that the most important part of any business is people - the need to build a team.

"Graeme put breakfast on for everyone at 7 o'clock in the morning, " his son says. "There were no MAF regulations - he would just go and grab some meat and make a big feed up for breakfast for everyone working in the factory - there'd also be a big lunch."

"It's pretty humbling. Look at what Graeme's created over the years, the new technologies brought into the industry, some of which have gone worldwide," Andy says.

One of those inventions is the halal stun box for cattle, now called the Jarvis electric stun box, which Lowe and his engineers developed and patented.

They also invented the technology of "hot boning" meat. "Basically you get rid of chillers," his son said. "Within 30 minutes of the animal being slaughtered, it is cut up into the different cuts ready for chilling. The old process used to take two or three days."

The new boning technology has saved the meat industry and farmers tens of millions of dollars annually, Andy Lowe says.

He feels it's an honour to carry on what his father started, although business has been tough in recent years.

"I just hope I can do as well as what he's done over the last 40 years."

Philanthropy was also a large part of Lowe's life. He sponsored the Hawke's Bay rescue helicopter for 20 years, the Hawke's Bay rugby union for more than 40 years and gave millions of dollars to local art and culture, civic facilities, sport, health, education, conservation and youth development.

He also started the Graeme Lowe Foundation, which supports education and medical equipment and research.

The family devote a lot of resources to conservation. Cape Sanctuary, driven by Andy and wife Liz, is the largest privately owned and funded wildlife restoration project of its kind in New Zealand.

"Graeme's always instilled in me that he's only got where he is in life through the support of the local community," Andy says.

"He's always taught me that giving back is very important."

+ Sources for this profile include Fairfax articles by Nick Krause and Marty Sharpe based on interviews with Andy Lowe and Margaret Baker, and from Craig Ellis' book Who Dares Wins Freedom and information supplied by Graeme Lowe himself.

Chapter Two

THE ZEN OF MANAGEMENT

These then are the things you will never learn in a text book. They are the insights which have been learnt by the country's top business leaders through sheer hard graft, sweat and tears.

They are, if you will, the Zen of Management. The 10 things you should know if you are to be a success in the business world at any level.

1. Plan for incremental growth.

The key responsibility for a leader is to determine the way forward – in business to decide what a company is going to be in the future, how it will be positioned, what products it will sell, how it will connect with its customers, what business model it will pursue. Deciding how to make that vision achievable and how the business will get from its current state to that beckoning future can be achieved in a range of ways - informal, broad brush-stroked intentions, or a complex and formalised annual planning process. The latter can involve multiple teams with established decision-making paths that produce strategic, tactical and operational goals dovetailed into lower level goals pursued by frontline teams that support the aims of those higher up the corporate ladder – a classic means-end chain..

One man who knew about charting a path forward, and the pitfalls that can await, is Tony Falkenstein. He was the youngest regional general manager for Polaroid at age 29 in the 1970s, led Optical Holdings in the 1980s from a share price of 38c to $12, founded Red Eagle Corporation, and now runs the $200m turnover Bartercard business, listed company Just Water International which sells water coolers into businesses and office furniture company Buro. He is one of the country's most respected entrepreneurs who gives backing and support to many up and coming business start ups and underwrote $300,000 to establish the country's first business school at Auckland's Onehunga High School .

21

He also donated $1 million of Just Water shares to the school and made similar donations to the University of Auckland Business School and the Unitec school of business management.

"The reason I want kids to understand business is I'd love them to be able to start without making the mistakes - of course daily you'll make little mistakes - but that you make them in context," he says.

What he means is that mistakes are unavoidable, even healthy, but they should be operational, and limited in scope and impact. Critically, they must be recoverable. But he worries that too many young business people start out thinking far too grandly, which immediately puts them at risk of mistakes that could see them go under.. Indeed, some are pursuing unachievable goals.

"I see a lot of kids going out there now and a lot of business plans where they really want to be the king pin immediately. They're putting everything into it and often wasting their years when they really have high energy on something which is just too big to do."

His advice is matched by that of Anne Norman, who with husband David Norman, grew a family business from seven small jewellery stores to a business empire which operates nine brands including the likes of Pascoes and Farmers, over 650 retail outlets and has approximately 10,000 employees in New Zealand and Australia. Again, Norman is someone who knows a thing or two about growth – and agrees it comes incrementally, with sound planning at each stage. She says the principles of graduated steps should be applied not just to growing a business but to planning your career.

"I would say to young people, that they need to realise that they are not going to start as the general manager. Every general manager, the best ones, work up the steps gradually and learn all the aspects of the business. I think kids can have an aspiration but you have to realise you have to go through that learning and the experience to get there."

She has a useful phrase - "learn and listen" – as you work through each stage and says the smart grasp every opportunity. "We are lucky in New Zealand because, generally speaking, when you are working here you do get lots of variety, whereas if you go to London you end up just doing one function. Don't be too narrow in your thinking because you never know when another avenue will open, another opportunity."

So the first word of wisdom is to take a stepped process in planned growth of a venture (or yourself) – always set challenging, stretch goals but fundamentally make them achievable so they establish a platform for growth in a sustainable and sensible way.

2. Roadtest

The advice of Falkenstein and Norman is echoed very much by Sir Stephen Tindall, the man best known as the founder of The Warehouse which he launched in 1982 with initial capital of $40,000, after a background of 12 years with retailer George Court & Sons. He floated The Warehouse Group in 1994 on the New Zealand Stock Exchange and it now has turnover of more than $1.5 billion with more than 85 red shed stores and almost 50 further stationery stores. What is less well known is that through his family Tindall Foundation and other vehicles he has acted as an angel investor who has put more than $150m in seed and venture capital into startup companies

This then is a man who knows about risk, about opportunity, and the importance of planning to avoid one and seize the other. His top tip to anyone starting out is "don't jump into things too quickly without researching them properly and road testing them. Sometimes you can go ahead with a venture too quickly. There is a lot of low cost testing you can do before pushing the button on taking a big risk."

3. Plan with integrity at the heart

Another advocate of more thoughtful growth is publishing magnate Dame Wendy Pye. She ran Shortland Publications, which was taken over by corporate raider Brierley Investments in 1985, and she subsequently lost her job. With characteristic determination, she launched her own Sunshine Books and became one of the world's largest producers of children's literacy material. Much of her thinking about business practice is grounded in an ethical approach and she agrees with Sir Stephen and Falkenstein on how to grow an enterprise - plan and take your time.

For her, any business plan must have strong values at its core.

"Build your business on the best integrity. Have sound principles of business. Sometimes it means probably slower growth than you want but it is built on very sound, not necessarily cautious, principles. It's not built on flashiness."

Another who stresses the same point is Douglas Goodfellow, one of New Zealand's wealthiest men, who built his business Amalgamated Dairies and managed a range of philanthropic endeavours. Into his 90s he ceded his office to son Bruce, but still kept an active hand on his interests from home. Goodfellow junior said of his father that his work ethic, a commitment to honest business dealings, became a hallmark which actually opened opportunity for him and assisted the business to grow.

"We had a very good profile and reputation out in the market as people to deal with. You needed honesty and integrity in business. Because of some of the shareholdings that he had he was approached to sell out at higher prices, but he would say, 'No, everybody's got to be treated fairly and all shareholders must receive the same price'."

You see here, and will see throughout this book, that the philosophical bent of these business leaders reflects both their background and the industry sectors they worked in. But woven together, there is an obvious underlying consistency in what they say.

4. Know when to shut up

Knowing when to shut up may seem an unusual piece of advice, but it's a hard-won tip offered up by Sir Rod Weir, a man who turned his back on a career working for others in 1963 to start his own business. He began as sole employee of his stock and station rural services company and by the time he retired 20 years later employed 4,400 staff. The company underwent a series of deals and acquisitions and is now PGG Wrightson, one of the giants of the country's rural sector.

His career has been based on selling – not just selling goods to farmers but also selling unity of purpose to staff, risk to financial backers and

Sir Rod Weir

visionary plans of growth to other business leaders as he forged his mergers and takeover deals. From the smallest sale to the biggest business punts, he knew the dynamics of each transaction intimately. His entire future at times hung upon these deals. So this is a man to listen to when he cuts away all the trimming and says simply at the heart of all business lies a sales process. We are all selling something to someone. That is the root of all business endeavour.

"I learnt through the stock and station business never ever oversell. I've seen so many transactions when the deal is almost complete or is complete and then the agent carries on and the proposed purchaser starts thinking about things he would otherwise never have thought of and starts to get cool on the deal and withdraws. So never, ever introduce something to a purchaser that he otherwise would never have thought of."

In short, he says: "Know when to shut up."

"I think it's terribly important not to oversell and to recognise when a transaction is a transaction."

And that salient advise can apply as equally to selling a product on a shop floor to convincing others of your argument in any situation – know when you are ahead, when to stop, when to back off. Pushing the advantage too hard, or without being sensitive to the mood of an issue, can all too quickly see it rebound on you.

5. Know those around you

The late Sir Wilson Whineray, the longest serving and arguably greatest captain of the All Blacks in the 1950s and 1960s, went from rugby to a Harvard University MBA. Then came a career in business which included chairman of the board of Carter Holt Harvey, one of the country's largest companies which swung some of the biggest deals of its time. His focus was very much on the personal character of the business person and you needed to listen when Sir Wilson talked about weighing and gauging character. This was a man who had depended, quite viscerally, on looking team mates in the eye and perceiving their strengths and ability both on the field and in the boardroom. Understandably therefore, one of his top tips was to understand in a real and meaningful way those who are closest around you, on whom you depend. Equally understandably he is a proponent of the EQ or Emotional Intelligence theories. You can, he said, tick off the various management skills or attributes "you go through the people and communication and goal setting and you're always left with something at the end of it that you say that doesn't quite add up there's something missing." That missing link is gut instinct. Dr. Peter Salovey of Yale University and John D. Mayer of the University of New Hampshire are credited with first developing the concept of "emotional intelligence" in 1990 though it was popularised by Daniel Goleman in his 1995 book, *Emotional Intelligence*. Sir Wilson agreed with it: "It's the feelings that you have about something and the feelings that you have about the people around you that are equally important to any other data you get. If something feels right, it probably is so long as the other stuff stacks up. To get those feelings in the right order you really need to know the people around you very well, to get to know how they feel about things and what their basic lifestyle and beliefs are. And when you really get to know the people around you, you will certainly know yourself by then and the whole process becomes rather easy."

Dame Wendy Pye agrees and says when assessing those you are going to be working or dealing with, look past the surface and assess what lies beneath. In a variation of the 'don't judge a book by the cover' she offers up the adage of don't judge by the marble flooring of the multimillion dollar mansions. She casts a jaundiced eye on those who favour conspicuous demonstrations of their wealth. "I always find it fascinating how people become flashy you know as soon as they become successful ... Are you trying to prove something to somebody?"

Used to doing business internationally, she has regularly rubbed shoulders with some of the old money of Europe and the USA and says you will rarely find gratuitous displays amongst them. "Its really funny how people judge people. People tend to judge people on the size of your house or whatever it is or someone lives somewhere. I know two very successful people in life and one is a very, very successful private banker who looks after some of the richest people in the world and he said to me one of the lessons he learnt in life which was really interesting, was 'never judge the marble floor or the pillars or the size of the car that people drive' . He says 'I learnt many years ago in banking they weren't the true people of the world' and I thought that was quite interesting and a good lesson in life. The other one, a very successful person today who is in New York city, very successful, said 'always deal the same way and treat your customers [the same way] whether they are a small buyer or a large buyer because the small buyer sometimes become the large buyer'."

6. Have broad social connections and a social consciousness

The advice of Sir Wilson and Dame Wendy relies on healthy doses of common sense applied to the many connections you make in your business life. Common sense, shrewdness, an ear attuned to the pitch of sensible business decisions, is a theme evident in everything the Business Hall of Fame laureates talk about. Closely allied to knowing

Sir Ron Carter

those around you in the business environment, , is ensuring you extend your circle of connections well outside your business focus. While building a business or a career within an existing business may be the major thrust of your life, there must be some balance and you should not neglect friendships and connections outside of your core business.

Sir Ron Carter, one of the founders of what is today Beca Group, Australasia's fastest growing and most successful engineering, architectural and design consultancy, said he had a "natural tendency to like and enjoy the company of other people irrespective of how successful they have been in an economic sense or any other way. I mean there's heaps of people that I know that have got values I greatly admire and who haven't got an aspiration to become wealthy but I envy aspects of their life."

"If you look at my close family friends they are people I have known, some since primary school days, some since secondary and university days, and none of those associations have been built out of any sort of commercial relationship. They are just our friends."

Indeed, such relationships outside of business can be vital in keeping executive stress and all the consequent health risks at bay. Sir Roderick Deane, formerly CEO of Telecom, a forrmer head of the State Services Commission and a key figure at the Reserve Bank, was renowned for working punishingly long days. Yet he advocates having a life outside business. "The arts and music and opera are great loves and these cultural activities are wonderful escapes into other worlds. They are like a therapy, reducing pressures and taking one into other spaces. Artists and musicians bring a magic to one's life." Typically, Deane extended his business acumen into these areas of personal passion. He was chairman of the national museum, Te Papa, for six years.

Another who exemplifies the benefits of wider horizons is Sir John Ilott. He died in 1973, one of the many deceased laureates you will encounter in this book., By looking back on the businesses they built and pulling together the strands of their life stories they provide almost perfect case studies, the embodiment of the principles espoused by the laureates interviewed. For his part Ilott built an advertising agency that helped cement some of the most powerful brand names of New Zealand's economic history - Edmonds, Dulux, Watties to name just a few. He was known affectionately as "The Dynamo" for the relentless attitude to work which had been drilled into him from an early age. But, critically, he also maintained a wide range of interests outside of work encompassing music, philosophy, trout fishing and stamp collecting.

His granddaughter Shona McKellar recalls: "He was a man of tremendous energy and interested in many different things. He was also extremely sociable and made friends all over the world. He was a far-sighted man with natural enthusiasm, energy and drive and worked well with people of all ranks."

In this he reflects both Sir Ron and Sir Roderick.

And these qualities in turn linked back to his business, helping to drive and seize opportunities when they arose. He was regarded as a "great innovator, motivator and expansionist."

Much has been written about this interaction between business and social concerns.. This can range from low-level corporate donation and sponsorship at one end to fully embracing the ethos of being a good corporate citizen'. Microsoft's Bill Gates energised the most recent debate on the issue in a controversial speech at the 2008 World Economic Forum in Davos. The forum is an independent international organization with the goal of improving the state of the world by engaging leaders in partnerships to shape global, regional and industry agendas. Gates' speech A New Approach to Capitalism in the 21st Century promoted the concept of 'creative capitalism' - where the vital, self serving vigour of capitalism is somehow fused with social goals.

Sir Ron: "I do think the emphasis that we should put onto business today and for the future is a great sense of social responsibility. I think to be successful over time you have to have brought success to other people and yourself and if society has got a future it's got to be one that embraces everybody not just a few winners."

Note a key part of this statement, 'over time.' As Jim Collins and Jerry Porras made clear in their book *Built to Last*, based on their research project at the Stanford University Graduate School of Business, all goals of businesses are only sensible if they focus on sustainability over time.

Regardless however, of how a company decides to tackle its corporate social responsibility, you as an individual business leader can, and should, demonstrate your own values in what you do. To borrow once more from Jim Collins, this time in his book about how companies achieve greatness, *Good to Great*, he drew a hierarchy of management competency describing the foremost Level Five executives as those who built enduring greatness through a paradoxical blend of personal humility and professional will. If we return then to Ted Lees, he wasn't just a business man. He engaged in local politics as a form of public service. Lees was an Auckland Harbour Board member from 1983–91, during which time major port reform took place. He also served on the World Wildlife Fund and the Hauraki Maritime Park Board and as president of his local Lions Club he led a project to establish a ground breaking retirement village in his community. He also served for 25 years as honorary Spanish consul for the North Island, for which he was knighted by the King of Spain, Juan Carlos, in 1997.

7. Communicate, communicate, communicate

The fluidity of the business environment has been mentioned – from global external economic and political trends, climate and sustainability issues, to internal pressures of a changing workforce, technology, and ultimately consumer needs and preferences. Such forces inevitably cause fundamental changes in the way business operates, from the organisation structure, to processes and deeper into the very mentality managers and workers must bring to the way they work. If you're only maintaining the status quo, your business will end up going backwards.

This was illustrated with Ted Lees facing the changes in primary processing in the 1950s to 1970s and is at the crux of the Learning Organisation model. Peter Senge based his book about Learning Organisations on the work at the Massachusetts Institute of Technology (MIT) which saw management in terms of systems dynamics. A business then is best seen within a physical, even organic, framework as a system which is flexible, evolving and constantly adjusting to conditions.

And inside that exists a corollary system – communication. New York's Hunter College Professor Joseph DeVito proposed seven "postulates of communication" (1985), one of which was that communication is a process of adjustment. It is a complex system in itself, with informational content and a relational context. If we carry on the organic metaphor, communication is the central nervous system within the business organism. However you view it, business and communication are deeply intertwined.

It is imperative for a leader at any level within an organisation to be informed. It is impossible to drive a learning culture through an organisation, to seek the ability for the company to react with the best decisions where needed, without building strong vertical, horizontal, communication into the very cellular structure of a business. In too many businesses workers and line managers at the coal face decry a lack of strategic understanding. Nothing creates greater stress or neuters effectiveness than a workforce which does not have a unified view of what to do , why and where they are going.

For Alan Burnet, a man who built the country's premier media empire, it is natural that his top tip for business is communication. He was immersed in an industry at the forefront of change working with one of the most disruptive change agents on the planet, Rupert Murdoch. Interestingly he faced off with Murdoch in a battle of wills at one point, and won, but more of that in a later chapter. Suffice to say at this point, Burnet swung a series of acquisitions that created Independent News Limited, which he led. It was part of the global Murdoch empire and ultimately sold in 2003 to Australia's Fairfax Media.

Burnet's words of wisdom on communication are delivered characteristically crisply and succinctly. "Communicate. Involve everyone that you are associated with, without in anyway breaking any confidences."

So great is the need for leaders to communicate, we return to it in more detail in a later chapter.

8. Be resilient, stubborn. Don't give up.

Underpinning all this is that you need the ability to see the long term shape of the business, a vision of the future which can comfortably withstand intermediary changes to the plan. In a way, it is not so much how you get there, so long as you do get there. It may seem contradictory when emphasising the need for flexibility and rapid fire decision making, but what that calls for is a resilient stubbornness. Vision needs execution. Clear strategic vision on company growth must be welded to an uncompromising attitude to seizing opportunity, a healthy appetite for risk, and a determined mindset to assimilate all changes that arise into the grand plan so that rather than causing the company to be thrown off course, they add to and enrich the model.

You find just such a philosophy in Sir Richard Carter, perhaps understandably so as he was a baron of the harvesting and exploitation of the primary resources of our country, a man whose business was so intimately linked to growth cycles of trees and fish. He was by necessity a man who had to take the long view. An accountant by trade, he was responsible for creating in 1985 what was then New Zealand's fourth-largest public company. Carter Holt Harvey, the merger of forester

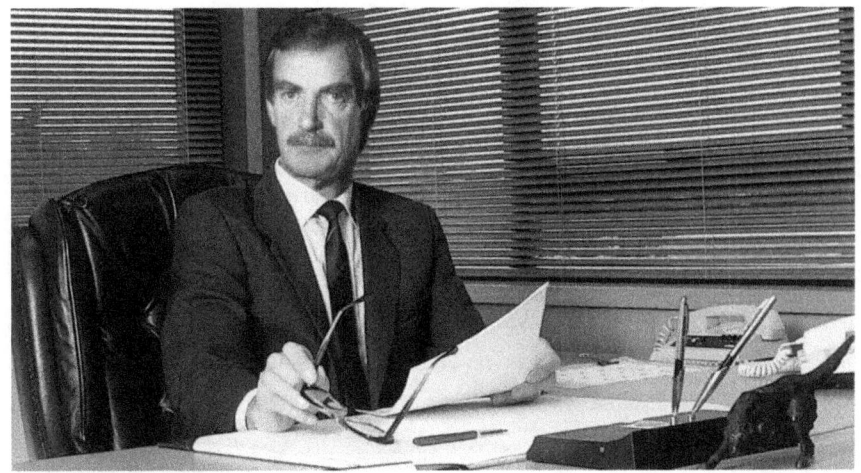

Sir Richard Carter

Carter Holt Holdings and manufacturer Alex Harvey Industries, became a group of international standing under Sir Richard's farsighted executive chairmanship. The merger, which the down-to-earth Sir Richard executed with his twin brother Ken, was one of several major deals that helped internationalise the group.

His tip then, made in the last major interview before he died in 2011: "Fortitude, stick in there, don't give up. Text books are fine I guess for some information and guidance as to what you might need to do in certain circumstances but there's no text book at all that can tell you in fact what to do and how to do it. This is where one can get a little cynical about MBAs and Harvard School of business and the rest of it. They're dealing with theoretical situations and training. Its not the upfront 'shot in the eye' that the students are really dealing with and I guess the ability to roll with the punches counts as much as anything."

A prime example of this persistence of vision lies in the creation of the fishing company Sealord. "Sealord was nothing when we became involved and to make it something we had to get government approvals to operate offshore fishing vessels, in this case Japanese. That involved basically years of argument and hassle and repeated interviews with ministers and members of parliament and the whole nine yards of beating against doors until we got our approvals. But again it was a case of sticking with it and not giving up and ultimately of course Sealord developed into a very successful international company."

None of which, however, should be confused with pigheadedness. Don't quit, is not a mantra for success if the fundamentals are wrong. In fact, many argue for fast failure if you've got it wrong and can't pivot the business into something more successful.

A sound business plan can withstand the vagaries of fortune but no amount of effort or money will make a poor product or flawed business model succeed in the long term. Therefore resilient determination has to be married to raw acumen to understand your business proposition.

9. Love your family

It may sound trite but a key message from the laureates is that you need a supportive family. Take Sir Roderick Deane when asked his secret of success: "My greatest skill was meeting Gillian and persuading her to marry me." And it is true, with working 60 hours plus a week, managers need supportive partners and family. When things at work are not going right, when the setbacks have you down, your family can be the fuel which recharges you. Deane again: "My daughter Kristen taught me to make the most of every day and to be positive about life no matter what the odds."

It is a little known fact that Deane's daughter has disabilities. "The IHC taught me how to work in leadership roles with large numbers of people without the trappings of power that come from high positions and in a mode which was much more democratic than I had typically experienced in the public service or corporate worlds. I helped the IHC, which is probably New Zealand's largest voluntary welfare organisation, to deliver on more normal inclusive lives for people with disabilities. There has been no more major achievement than this in my life."

This need for family backing has also helped Sir Graeme Douglas build his pharmaceutical business: "You have to have support from the home front of course, that's obligatory, otherwise you have always got a problem."

Ted Lees is a man renown for the entertaining and enjoyable way he recounts his past, extraordinary exploits, a man with whom you can easily lose a few hours as you revel in his company. On this point he is uncharacteristically pithy: : "Find a good wife."

10. Know Thyself

Much of what the business laureates talk about revolves around judgement. Drawing up plans, striking deals, forging relationships, communicating effectively, showing the strength of character to push issues through – all of this requires the exercise of judgement, the foundation of which is enough self awareness to make the right choices for you, your colleagues and your company.

Perhaps then, this is The Number One Tip. Know yourself. And your motivations. Why do you want to be a manager, a leader, an owner of a business? Do you like directing staff? Do you like the prospects of big pay packets, company car and perks? Do you have ideas that you want to pursue, do you want to change the world?

"You have to look at your own personality," says Tony Falkenstein. "I found at 29 I was general manager at Polaroid and from then I sort of thought I quite like being the boss. And in fact I want to be the boss. I like being the boss and therefore I don't like partners. Not because I don't get on with people but I have a lot of self confidence that 'hey what I'm doing is right.'"

Much as you may want to be the person in charge, ask yourself whether you have the personal traits that will make you successful. For instance, do you have an appetite for risk?

Sir Richard Carter had blunt advice on this: "So long as you have the fundamentals of a sound business model, there is no need to panic. Nothing changes in terms of how you go about things. That's really I suppose the important thing. People can write all sorts of books and produce fancy ideas, technology changes can introduce new things, but the fundamentals are still the same. You have to decide if you are going to spend your money or not. And if you're not good at that, you're going to be a failure – be that as an investor or an owner operator or a manager."

You also need commitment and the drive. Being a manager can mean punishingly long hours, it can mean shouldering risk and responsibility and along with the plaudits for getting it right, there are the concordant consequences of getting it wrong.

"The one lesson is that in the end, or at the start, it all comes back to you. The old 'I'm the master of my fate, I'm the captain of my soul,'" says Sir Wilson Whineray.

No amount of reading management and leadership books, picking up qualifications, writing of memos and reports, counts if you lack a fundamental quality of character, which he describes as "push and drive."

"Are leaders made or born? There is no answer to that but I do think some people are born that have a little bit more of a push to get on. They get on a confidence treadmill. Obviously during life not everything goes your way. You get knocked over and you can stay knocked over or you can dust yourself off, pick yourself up."

Many self improvement books refer to internal dialogues and techniques to strengthen a positive attitude. All of which has merit, but fundamentally, you need to be honest with yourself about who you are, says Dame Wendy Pye. She has a very centred self awareness herself, an international businesswoman on a world stage, who yet describes herself as a housewife. "I basically like to go home and we grow our own vegetables and I love to cook and I make jams and chutneys. I am a very practical housewife, I love that part of my life," she says. "Why would I need to impress anybody?"

All this means understanding your limitations and your strengths and what your platform for growth should be. The flip side though is don't undersell yourself – have horizons.

The Top Ten Tips

1. Plan sustainable incremental growth not big bang heroics

2. Roadtest

3. Put integrity at the heart of what you do

4. Know when to shut up

5. Know those around you

6. Have broad social connections and a social consciousness

7. Communicate, communicate, communicate

8. Be resilient, stubborn. Don't give up.

9. Love your family

10. Know thyself

SUMMARY

The country's top business leaders have shared unparalleled access to their thinking about what makes good leaders and good businesses tick. Perhaps the last word should be left with Ted Lees – an engineer to the heart, he expresses his view in simple, mechanical terms. "Always source the best components."

And that truly sums it up, when you look at the wide, almost philosophical definition of components he is using. Put into your life, into your career, the best quality inputs in everything you do, be it work, rest or play – the best knowledge, thinking, will power, team members, colleagues, , friends, and partner. Go for quality, don't shortchange your customer, but also don't shortchange yourself.

GEORGE SAMUEL BECA: Designing Innovation

Consult a management text book and you will find the model for business success presented in crisp, logical terms.

Understand your client, produce products and services that connect with their needs, innovate, add value, and exceed their expectations. In concentrating on your client, you may also find you transform your company so that it becomes far more flexible, creative and enduring.

Yet the simplicity of concept is so often compromised and lost in execution for many companies.

During less buoyant economic times it is vital to clear away the clutter and understand the core business which success, even survival, depends upon. It is also timely to reflect on a business leader who implicitly understood the fundamentals of good business and, more importantly, managed to weld it into the fabric of the company he built.

George Beca, CBE DFC, (1921–2001) is just such an example.

Beca, along with Sir Ron Carter who features throughout this book, were the visionary thinkers from the 1950s through to the 1980s who created the modern Beca Group. It is the country's largest New Zealand-owned professional services company and one of Australasia's leading engineering consultancies.

Beca joined the two-man Auckland engineering practice of Gray & Watts in 1952 and two years later was made a partner. As chairman and managing director he presided over the 1968 amalgamation of Beca Carter, as the firm had become, to form Beca Carter Hollings & Ferner. He retired in 1986.

The Beca Group now employs more than 2000 and operates in 41 countries.

At the heart of the Beca success was his commitment to his customers.

"He was very innovative in looking for solutions for client's needs, how to add value to what he was doing for them. He wouldn't have called it innovation though, to him it was a commitment to service," says Gavin Cormack, former executive chairman of Beca.

Pioneering design and innovative solutions quickly became the Beca trademark. A stand out example was the pavilion designed in the 1950s for Auckland's Ellerslie race course. Half a century on, it still stands out as being special. Though the look may these days seem muted, the engineering behind remains impressive, one of the world's first structures to use tubular steel cantilever space frames anchored to a central core.

There were a host of other examples, many less glamorous, more functional in nature. Cormack talks of the mile long potlines at the Tiwai Point aluminium smelter built in precast prestressed concrete – again a world first. "I, as a young engineer, was responsible for this design but it was George Beca who saw the added value and pushed Comalco so hard that this technology was eventually accepted."

And in what could almost be seen as a text book market-pull phenomenon (think Peter Drucker), this focus on the client inevitably flowed through to changes in the way the company was organised and operated - to its very DNA.

It may be unkind, but it has been said that before Beca came along engineers were a dull lot. Under his leadership however, engineers moved to the centre of large multi-disciplinary projects. In the early

1960s Beca began promoting engineers as principal advisors, ultimately, that changed the Beca Group's profile from a structural and civil engineering company to a full service consultancy. From being price takers, the engineer became the pivotal manager in the process, determining projects and injecting creativity.

The innovative way the Beca Group perceived and positioned itself flowed through to the wider engineering profession. Beca worked hard to lift the profession's standing through the foundation of the New Zealand Association of Consulting Engineers and by persuading successive governments to engage engineering consultants to foster design innovation. Under his leadership and stewardship New Zealand engineers took on the world.

While we call the Beca story an innovative one, importantly it is a reframing of the concept of innovation. Rather than one off, paradigm changing eurekas, its innovation process was more incremental and sustainable. It was about cultural and operational change which ensures that creativity and working for novel solutions becomes embedded in a business. It becomes integrated innovation that is second nature and may not even be consciously recognised as active 'innovation' by a company.

On this issue, Cormack says innovation became part of normal, everyday activity at Beca. Furthermore, he said that "it was the environment created by George Beca and then followed on and reinforced by Sir Ron Carter that has led to many opportunities for innovation and advancement. Their encouragement of teamwork and technical excellence, their total commitment to clarifying risk, and to managing that risk, is a legacy."

Eldest son John says one of his father's greatest strengths was "fostering development of people and innovation and expansion." On expansion, John Beca says his father critically understood the vulnerability of a firm dependent on the New Zealand market; he had experienced tough economic times and saw the value of expanding overseas.

Global diversification is the great need of so many New Zealand businesses, and yet like the basic fundamental of business, one which is too often flawed in execution. And again, with Beca, we see absolute success. Today close to 40 per cent of the company's revenue comes from outside New Zealand.

Economist Brian Easton says Beca exemplifies an export category frequently overlooked in public discussion, New Zealanders applying their professional skills overseas.

The achievement of George Beca is testament to his drive and energy shown in his wider background.

The son of a draper from Putaruru, Beca was just 18 when he joined the Royal New Zealand Air Force in October 1939. It was the start of an audacious military career, second only to his business career.

He flew in North Africa, then from Britain on bombing raids over Germany, but one of his finest exploits came in Burma where his superb airmanship earned him the DFC. He later flew in the Pathfinder Squadron, which selected only the best flyers.

Beca returned to New Zealand a war hero but instead concentrated on becoming a test pilot. He enrolled in an engineering degree at Auckland University College where his professor recognised his managerial talent and recommended he become a civil engineer.

He was a man of his war time generation who missed out on four years of civilian life but became engrained with the ability to learn quickly, be adaptive and to move fast to get ahead. No matter what his profession, you sense this is a man who would have done well in anything he took on.

John Beca sums his father up thus: "He was driven; he was generous with his time, incredibly principled and a very moral person from a business practice point of view. He was very strong on accountability and responsibility. He was comfortable in a leadership role. In many ways his strength was as a leader and a manager."

Cormack agrees, saying a vital element of the Beca character was a strong ethical stance.

When Beca retired his talents were publicly recognised in 1991 when he was made a CBE for services to engineering and the community and in 2000 when he, was awarded one of the first honorary doctorates in engineering by the University of Auckland – at his side as fellow recipients of the honour, Sir Ron Carter and Tom Schnackenberg. He also received civil engineering fellowships in New Zealand, Australia and Britain.

+ Sources for this profile include business journalist and historian Graeme Hunt, the Beca Group, Gavin Cormack in his Hopkins Lecture of 2005 and other speeches, and interviews by David Gadd with the Beca family

ANNE AND DAVID NORMAN: Reviving retail

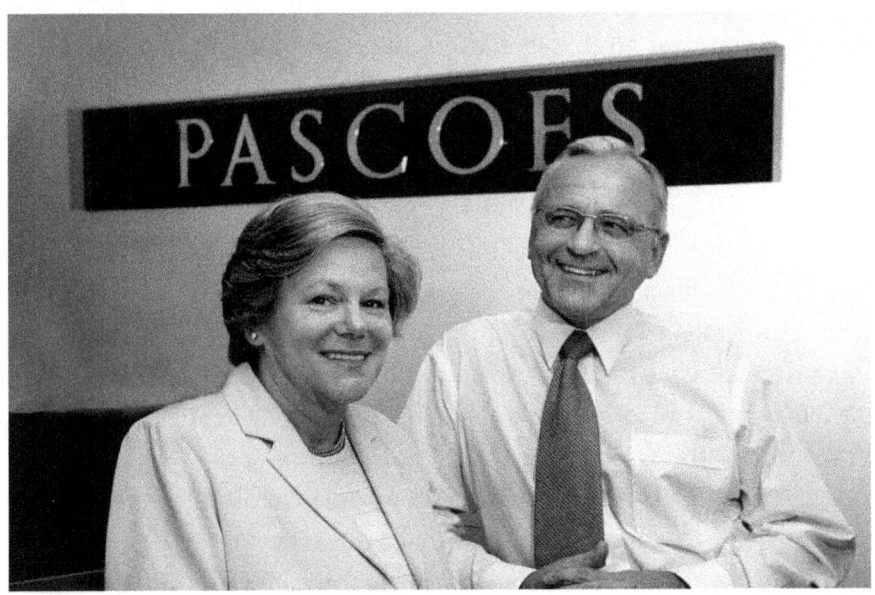

There was only one question which made David and Anne Norman wince and grimace during our interview with them. It had nothing to do with their retail empire James Pascoe Group, which now has almost 11,000 employees here and across the ditch. It wasn't whether or not they would stock the controversial book about Macsyna King, mother of dead twins Chris and Cru Kahui. Nor was it about their thoughts on religion. The question which drew a gasp and furrowed their brows was whether the All Blacks would snatch the Rugby World Cup in 2011.

That's not to trivialise any of the above, rather it illustrates their fierce patriotism. They were at every All Black match of that World Cup campaign, having bought two packages themselves before finding they were invited to most of the team's games anyway.

"Is this our year? It's so nerve- racking - I can't imagine the strain those players must be under though, " Anne said. "It's like the netball the other night. It's going to be as tense as that."

Husband David, who usually works most of his week in Australia, felt we could be lacking a bit of the Australian "mongrel". "It's the one thing I do like about working in Australia - it's [about being] tough, when you get going when someone says 'no, you can't do that', " he said. "The problem with the All Blacks is every time they play another team, it's the other team's final and they know they've got to win."

In the end of course, it was our year, and it was not the old foe Australia who risked upsetting our dream, but France. Still David Normans' comments about the Australian attitude when in an underdog scenario are worth noting — because the Normans have applied a fair bit of Australian pugnaciousness in their approach to business, particularly in taking Australian failure and turning it into Kiwi success. They have repatriated two companies from Australian ownership. They bought Kiwi department store icon Farmers in 2003 and Whitcoulls and Borders from administrators in 2011. Their group, with sales of $2 billion a year, specialises in picking up distressed companies and then nursing them back to health, but not without thorough due diligence.

The pair originally eyed Australian-based Prouds Jewellery in 1989 when it got into financial trouble but it was six years before they bought that chain out of administration. Their next big play was buying Farmers. The original discussion was the result of an approach by Farmers to discuss having Pascoes jewellery kiosks in its stores.

Whitcoulls, founded in Christchurch in 1882 as Whitcombe & Tombs, was a different matter. The Normans were approached by a broker and a bank before the chains went into administration and declined. But, as Anne points out, where would New Zealand be without Whitcoulls? There was also the matter of 900 staff.

"Anne and I are passionate New Zealanders and although we do recognise that on the world stage we are but tiny players, this doesn't mean we should lose our identity, " David said. "We certainly intend to tailor the Whitcoulls product offer, as we do with all of our other divisions, for the Kiwi market."

The chains' former owner, private equity parent REDgroup, failed because it treated New Zealand as another state of Australia and dispensed with its local buying team, he said.

"That's expecting a New Zealand woman to use an Australian cookbook, a Kiwi man to support Australian sporting icons and it's just not going to happen, " David said.

He said the company was typical of a run-down business. A massive amount of maintenance and equipment replacement was needed. The core IT system was outdated and heavily patched and required major work, particularly around the accounts area. The pay system was also unreliable and saw staff unpaid at times. REDgroup also failed to appreciate that the cost of shipping goods from Auckland to Christchurch was the same as sending them from Sydney to Auckland. The distribution centre was "extremely tired" and the range and volume of product had halved in some stores, particularly during voluntary administration in 2011.

There remained however a wonderful sense of passion for the brand, Anne said, mirroring the affinity Kiwis have for Farmers and Pascoes, founded by Anne's grandfather James Pascoe in 1906.

David points out the business repatriated a chunk of its earnings to New Zealand through a transfer pricing policy negotiated with our IRD and the Australian Tax Office. For the last few years that's been around $20 million, which is taxed in New Zealand. "We've very much got the tax department on our side fighting for our cause because we have to renegotiate this every five years and the Aussies hate it," said David.

The couple have eschewed media attention for most of their careers, so it is not surprising they are reluctant to reveal their political leanings. Judiciously, David said they have always felt a need to be publicly apolitical and "non- religious".

The question of religion arose only because of the benevolence of some of their actions, such as continuing to pay 200 staff in Christchurch full wages after the earthquakes and doing the same for a slightly smaller number in Queensland following flooding there. The couple also fought hard to ensure no one lost their job in the Whitcoulls purchase.

David is a lapsed Baptist and admits he still holds to the church's teachings "in terms of honesty, integrity". Anne's great-great-great-grandfather the Rev John Churton was the first vicar of St Paul's

Anglican Church - since demolished - in Auckland. "The 10 Commandments are a good basis for life I believe," she said.

The pair are active philanthropists, primarily supporting the Leukaemia & Blood Foundation. Each has lost siblings to leukaemia-related disease. The company has committed to a corporate gift of $1 million over four years. Additionally, the University of Auckland's faculty of medical and health sciences offers an annual $15,000 grant, the Anne and David Norman Fellowship in Leukaemia and Lymphoma Research.

Farmers has also promoted World Lymphoma Awareness day through its stores and participated in Shave for a Cure. In its centenary year, 2009, the company and its customers raised $2m for charity through national gold coin appeals. That appeal raised $480,000 for tsunami relief in Samoa and Tonga.

Anne doesn't like discussing group earnings, principally because it might paint an image of piles of money in the bank. That's not the case, she explained - the number of stores and staff require a lot of capital. "There's a lot of money tied up here. We have close to 11,000 staff now and we reinvest back into the companies," she said. "We do it to give staff good working conditions and customers the stock that needs to be there. Retail stores are extremely cash-hungry."

There's another stand-out feature with the Normans - they're net buyers, business accumulators. "We've never sold a business - we don't even sell properties, " David said.

As to the book on Macsyna King which inspired 48,000 people to join a Facebook group calling for it to be banned from all bookstores. David's biggest concern was for staff, many of whom fear the protesters "because some of them have been quite vitriolic already". "That's the vexed question - do you give in to a vocal minority?" David said.

"You don't," Anne replied.

+ Sources for this profile were a one to one interview with Anne and David Norman by Nick Krause

Chapter Three

LEADERSHIP - WHAT IT REALLY TAKES

During the great implosion of the 2008 Global Financial Crisis, in New Zealand alone, thousands of investors lost billions of dollars to stupidity, cupidity, recklessness and greed.

US-based multinational Goldman Sachs was reviled as one of the banks at the heart of the complex financial derivative trades which imploded, helping to send the world shuddering into deep recession. Yet senior Goldman executives seemed to shrug off any culpability. In a 2009 interview with London's Times newspaper, chief executive Lloyd Blankfein delivered a perfect example of how not to handle public relations when he described himself as just a banker "doing God's work". Other leading financiers, albeit with less hubris than this wizard of Wall Street, also ducked blame.

Amid the recriminations and justifications, multi-millionaire New Zealand entrepreneur Dame Wendy Pye cut through the obfuscation and the opprobrium to pin point the fundamental issue. What we saw during the collapse was, said Dame Wendy, lack of leadership, both here and overseas.

In business, when mistakes are made, the buck stops with the boss: "But I don't see many managers standing up and acting as role models. Too many of our CEOs and Boards are just trying to hide behind subterfuge."

It was always "nebulous macro issues" which were used to explain failures after the GFC – and even now, many business leaders use the same tactics to evade responsibility for poor performance. But as Dame Wendy sees it, the tough economic terrain, the international issues buffeting us were not, and are still not, the whole story. After all, she says, we all face the same economic conditions, and not all of us fail. "Shouldn't you blame yourself also?" she asked of our business leaders.

Dame Wendy said what many thought. And she was well-placed to comment. She has suffered setbacks: in 1985, she was shocked to be

Dame Wendy Pye

suddenly dumped as a divisional manager of the now-defunct NZ News group. Within 24 hours, she had decided to launch her own business, and over the next 25 years, took her Sunshine Book and Galaxy Kids brands into worldwide publishing, including providing television and online content in 21 countries. She became one of the country's richest businesswomen, at one stage worth an estimated $60m. It was a business built on her own investment: no public float, no government handouts.

And Dame Wendy took huge, calculated risks, and openly admits to making huge mistakes, including a failed partnership with a US distributor that cost her dearly. Her business has seen good years and bad. And the buck has always stopped at her door. She exemplifies the best of leadership.

The raw, intangible quality of leadership is just one component of the management mix required to run a successful company, but it is perhaps the most important. It involves not just an array of techniques and taught skills, it exposes the essence of a person - their integrity, authenticity, ability to shine, to influence others. And because leadership is so personal, it is not the exclusive domain of those holding formal management positions within an organisation. Leaders can be seen on the factory floor, in office cubicles, or the field, without holding official status. US lawyer and leadership coach Robin Sharma has a useful term for this – leadership without title, meaning leadership qualities are often inherent, a part of a person's moral and ethical fibre, baked into their DNA. For these people, their natural tendency to lead will shine through. Even in the schoolyard, primary school teachers will tell you they can spot potential leaders.

Does this innate nature mean leadership is simply charisma? No, it's more than that. Jim Collins, in his book *Good To Great*, draws a sharp distinction between the celebrity chief executive, with the big personality and penchant for making headlines, and the truly successful leader. For the latter Collins coined the term Level 5 Leader and characterised them with qualities such as being modest, self-effacing and workmanlike; in his words, "more plough horse than show horse". A forceful, flashy charismatic personality can get you a long way, but ultimately, true leadership must be backed by substance. More important than personality power is the ability to deliver, which can only be achieved by committed, focused and determined work.

So what must a leader deliver?

While the characteristics of leadership itself are hard to define, being highly individualistic in style with few clear rules, there is consensus around what a leader must deliver – it can be filtered to just one goal, one deliverable: sustainable success. For a senior leader in a public company, success may be defined as maximising shareholder value; for a private company, it's perhaps simple profit maximisation, in a charity it will be ensuring revenues consistently outweigh outgoings so the organisation has certainty it can continue its philanthropic endeavours.

However success is defined, there must be an authenticity to how it is achieved. For a business leader success must be built on the back of sustainable practices to produce goods or services people want to buy and are worth more in the market than they cost to produce. If this sustainable success were replaced with short-term profit-taking or cost-cutting, a company would have little likelihood of long-term survival. For without a focus on sustainability, a company is necessarily focused on the vicissitudes of immediate needs, unable to adequately plan strategically to position itself for the future of its market (whether that be a future driven by changing consumer preferences, rival competitiveness or disruptive technology requiring new business models) or to promote the innovative and adaptable culture on which long-term success depends.

If we agree the responsibility for this falls to the leader, they are, then, critical to the business' bottom line. And when we look at leadership in practice in the real world, we see the best leaders display many variations in style and philosophy, but they are underpinned by the same base. They concentrate their leadership talents on the following three key areas:

- Creating shared visions and setting direction for their businesses – they identify opportunities and set goals to exploit such opportunities;
- Getting the structure right to achieve their aims, and putting the right people in the right place;
- Establishing the right environment for those right people to flourish.

Rarely can leadership be taught. But managers, particularly where they are responsible for heading a team, and most particularly at senior level, must be both competent and have within them demonstrable leadership traits. Examining the shared wisdom of the business laureates of the Fairfax Media Hall of Fame offers salient lessons that can show the way forward.

SHARE THE VISON - SET THE DIRECTION

In business, somebody has to be at the top, to make the decisions, decide the way forward, call the shots and be held accountable to directors, shareholders or owners.

But nobody can do it alone. Not even a company seemingly inseparably identified with an individual CEO (think Apple and Steve Jobs) truly operate solely at the command of one person. Businesses are social entities. So a leader galvanizes a team to deliver on company objectives, to adhere to rigorous commercial discipline and make its product or service the best it can possibly be.

They must do this, or their legacy on leaving will be, at the least, turmoil and stagnation, at worst irreparable decline. So to lead effectively, the leader must clearly set out the path they want the company to travel, identify what they want to achieve, explain to people what they expect of them, what they are accountable for, and give those people the opportunity to achieve their potential.

Two men who know about leadership at the highest level offer incisive definitions: "Leadership is about providing people clarity of purpose and vision, committing them to identify with and focus on that purpose and vision and then energising them to individually and collectively drive continuously to achieve them. That's the role of the leader as I see it."

That's the view of Hugh Perrett, who was managing director of FoodStuffs NZ, which – through the New World and Pak'N Save chains - controls more than half the weekly grocery spend of New Zealand families. (For more on Hugh Perrett, see his Profile.)

Perrett says that to be successful in business, you need "shared values and harmony so that everyone gets on well, everyone pulls in the same direction through core values and ideology and operating philosophies. It is very important for people to have those at a common level."

Then there is the view of Sir Roderick Deane, former head of Telecom, once the country's most significant public company with more than 2,500 staff: "I like people working with me to have a clear understanding of where we are heading, a vision if you like; to have clear written objectives - 4 or 5 at most, written on only a page or two - to assume individual accountability for delivering on those objectives and to be appropriately rewarded for achieving the goals."

We see here that the leader sets the strategic direction for where the business needs to go – perhaps through consensus and consultation, or rigorous and disciplined dissection of market data, or maybe, in rare cases, individual genius. That's only the first step. Just as critically, they must then ensure their message reverberates throughout the organisation. Leadership has a vital component of communication, whether it be as Deane epitomises, working through a hierarchical tree

A pivotal thinker at the Reserve Bank under Prime Minister Rob Muldoon, Sir Roderick Deane became in quick succession Chief Economist, then Deputy Governor of the bank in 1982. He is credited as a driving force of one of the greatest paradigm shifts in the country's business history – moving from Keynesian-style intervention and state planning toward a greater reliance on markets and stable monetary and fiscal policy. Under the Labour Government of David Lange he headed the State Services Commission, then Telecom.

of structural management, delivering succinct, measurable goals to top managers who then pass the call to action and the ethos to their direct reports and onwards down the chain of command, or via a more personal rallying as Perrett expressed with his desire to light fires and energise.

Whatever the method, a critical aspect of communication is that it is a two-way process. Language experts will define it as a dynamic transactional process – in simpler terms, an interaction; even for the man or woman at the top. The heart of communication isn't to tell, dictate, lecture, instruct or demand – it is to share and exchange information, to motivate and to influence behaviour. Leaders listen. Good leaders listen exceptionally well - and learn. Smart leaders pick up feedback where they can, they digest and integrate what they have heard into their internal decision-making process, adapting their approach and execution, and sometimes even their goals, because of what they have learned.

It is useful to reflect here on a report by American academics

John Robert Stewart and Carole Logan from 1993 which emphasises just how hard it is to listen well, highlighting the effort that good leaders put into this deceptively simple task. Using tests of recall, they showed people typically remember only about 25 per cent of the information they hear.

A classic, and natural, exemplar of this is Sir Ron Carter, a man whose particular skill in leadership was his ability to interact with people. Don't underrate that as a soft skill. It is a vital component of leadership and management.

Sir Ron: "I've always respected the knowledge of other people and I want to know what they think, in order to build my own knowledge up on any subject. I have always been a believer of the amount of knowledge that exists in society in very ordinary people, people who are themselves not being spectacular, but they will have knowledge that is useful. I've always tried to encourage people to tell me what they think. That leads to a respect for me. They've chosen to follow and recognise me as a leader. They feel I will pay attention to their views and try to accommodate them. It almost might be a friendship. I actually really like people. I like to number my friends across the community at any level of success and perhaps that's a quality [of leadership.]"

Anne Norman brings a further interesting aspect to this discussion. She, with partner David Norman, has built a reputation for buying into ailing businesses and turning their fortunes around. Her forte is retail – Farmers and Whitcoulls being prime examples of chains the pair have revived. Retail is something engrained in her. She will tell you "I think women like to shop don't they" but that self deprecation disguises an iron eye and grasp on the fundamentals of retail built from lifelong exposure to the family business Pascoes founded by her grandfather. Frequently the answers to success existed within the failing business all the time, she says – it was just unrecognised. This was because it lay with the staff on the shop floor. "If you go into a store, often the staff will have the answers. They've just been getting bad direction from the people at the top." So in her experience it is senior managers who can in fact hinder the flourishing of a company – because they fail to tap into, and listen to, the acumen sitting with their own workforce.

Some leaders, like Norman and Sir Ron Carter, are intimately connected with their business, steeped in its lifeblood from years of service within the companies they helped build from the ground up, and discussion with those at the coalface is typically a discussion between equals in terms of the technical expertise.

Sir Rod Weir is of the same persuasion. He, perhaps controversially, believes this innate understanding of the technical aspects of a business is crucial for strong, competent leadership.

"I became the managing director and chairman of the company, but I did know and understand the business very well indeed and I wouldn't ask any of the staff to do a job that I wasn't prepared to do myself. So my belief in leadership style is to have a very deep knowledge of the business and to make sure that when you ask someone to do something, you know what they're doing and what you've asked them to do."

There are, however, professional managers, or those who transfer to a company from other industries, who rely more on general principles of practical and theoretical management to guide how they lead a company. And that is perfectly valid. But it reinforces the deeper relevance of two-way communication, of listening to those who must carry out the commands of top management, must translate a corporate vision from polished prose and printed text to the realities of products shipping out of warehouses and meeting customer needs.

It also highlights that, regardless of whether a leader has come through the ranks or joined a company in a management role, they need to be close to the business to be truly effective. They have to understand its dynamics intimately; have to know the key levers that affect it. While, theoretically, there is a similarity between all businesses in the crude understanding of the disciplines and parameters of production, distribution, market demand, supply and customer relations, there are deeply important nuances in every industry, and even within individual businesses competing within each sector. There is real danger for leaders at every level, particularly for those in senior corporate level posts, that they become trapped in the office, divorced from the real world of the business they lead.

Every company has formal channels reflecting the chain of command, but a wise manager steps aside from this – carefully achieving a balance, so they do not undermine their line managers, but always appreciating the need to take the time to test the temperature at all levels of their business.

Sir Rod Weir, even with his deep roots in the business he had created, was always conscious of the risk of isolation within the C-Suite offices, and strove to remain connected "by talking regularly, by ringing the managers early in the morning and at night and calling on them as often as you can, and seeing as many clients as possible.

"The higher up the ladder you get, the harder this becomes – but you have to keep in very close touch with the business and know where it's heading and what it's doing." Textbooks give it a term, MBWA – management by walk-about – where a leader is seen on the factory floor, amongst the office cubicles, communicating, talking his vision. And listening to the feedback, antennae alert for problems and potentials.

Indeed, it has been argued that smart corporate managers wanting to understand how their companies really tick need to seek out the malcontents and marginalised workers in the firm.

John Van Maanen, a sociology professor from the Massachusetts Institute of Technology, is the master of researching corporate culture, having made his name in the 1970s with pioneering studies of American and British police, Atlantic fishermen and Disneyland staff. He studied workers by living with them, like an anthropologist amongst third world tribes, creating as he did so the discipline of organisational ethnography.

Every company, he says, has workers on the outer and they are a source of valuable insight. "As organisations grow and the distance between senior management and the people who are doing the work becomes so extreme, senior managers live in a world that really is quite different, and they see a world which is in some way fantasy." But it is vital for managers to have a realistic view of their company and often the people who really know and – most importantly – would give an honest answer free of self-serving political agendas, are the marginalised.

Managing people can make you smarter

Dr Michael Valenzuela, head of Regenerative Neuroscience at Australia's University of New South Wales School of Psychiatry is a leader in research into "brain plasticity", or the brain's ability to repair, rewire and regenerate itself.

In 2011 he found evidence that managing other people at work triggers structural changes in the brain, protecting its memory and learning centre well into old age. Valenzuela's research team identified a link between managerial experience in a person's working life and the integrity and identified a link between managerial experience in a person's working life and the integrity and larger size of a person's hippocampus - the area of the brain responsible for learning and memory. He said the findings refine our understanding of how staying mentally active promotes brain health, potentially warding off diseases such as Alzheimer's.

"We found a clear relationship between the number of employees a person may have supervised or been responsible for and the size of the hippocampus. This could be linked to the unique mental demands of managing people, which requires continuous problem solving, short-term memory and a lot of emotional intelligence, such as the ability to put yourself in another person's shoes. Over time this could translate into the structural brain changes we observed," Valenzuela said.

"Often people who are marginal ... are freer to talk and may have greater insight rather than a perfectly accepted central person in the organisation who is perfectly happy with that organisation's culture," says van Maanen. "Companies can learn from these sub-cultures. I think these sub-cultures have a lot to offer - because they see things in a different way, they are often sources of really brilliant ideas."

A leader, then, defines direction. A strong leader communicates well, ensuring the direction they set has been informed with the best possible input, including talking to their executive team and key operational people wherever they may be within the company hierarchy.

And if that was all a leader did, they would be hopeless. No amount of strategic vision of where a company should position itself is worthwhile without being allied to the ability to make it happen. This leads to two further considerations. The first is the public efforts of bringing the wider company with you while pursuing your strategic direction. The second is the more private wrestling with the demons of decision-making.

To make it happen, the leader needs to first set a demanding pace, with plenty of stretch goals, high performance aspirations and the remuneration mechanisms and motivating culture to ensure everyone delivers. Often this involves being uncompromising. Always it should focus on lifting your team.

Hugh Perrett again: "You need to have the ability to energise other people, and by that I mean to get them to do and achieve, because they want to, what they normally wouldn't be capable of doing or achieving. I think you need to have courage, that's very important, because courage is really about taking risks. It's about taking and accepting responsibility, it's about being prepared to be accountable and about putting yourself on the line. And that might seem not too difficult but there are a lot people who really can't do that."

Risk takes us to that second consideration. It is a key word for any leader. A leader must make decisions, and decision-making always revolves around the weighing and balancing of opportunity versus risk. No amount of communication, data-gathering or analysis can deflect from the fact that a leader must ultimately decide on and commit to a course of action. This alone can decide whether you are built to be a leader or not. Sir Richard Carter expresses it well when he says: "Everybody's perception of risk is different, of course, and I guess a lot of it is related to the amount of intestinal fortitude one might have in deciding what risk you can wear and what you can't. And most of it, of course, is intangible."

Those intangibles include consequences which when dealing with major decisions, be it in a small company or a major corporate, can cost serious money, jobs, the leader's own job or even the company's own survival.. And because the act of staring risk in the face and believing the promise of reward outweighs the risk, is so central to the act of leadership, it is an area most leaders talk about. Here is a selection of what our leaders have said on the issue.

Sir Wilson Whineray: "There are many different leadership styles and … I don't know that we consciously set about having a style. It's what emerges from our experiences and tasks along the way, so as I reflect what I think my leadership style was, it was probably that I was fairly collegial, communicative, embracing of people around me and fairly open. But in the end, it always falls pretty much to one person to make the decision. I don't suggest for a minute my style was one of committees deciding on what was going to happen or majority votes …for serious matters, one person has to make the decision and set about implementing it."

Hugh Perrett: "Underlying toughness is another important factor and by that I mean that you have the ability to operate effectively even under severe stress or quite adverse situations, that you don't get thrown out of gear by that."

Sir Roderick Deane: "I am not a handwringer; I consult and decide and get on with it. That is how change and improvement comes to pass."

Pulling these many threads together, we see the context in which the executive leader operates. They must often have a helicopter level view of their business, seeing the big picture, balancing the jarring immediacy of risk with the longer opportunity of growth and development, the macros and the competitive environment. It is only within this wider horizon that adequate goals and true direction can be set.

Yet those decisions must be informed with the realities of the business itself. A leader has to dive into the detail, to reach down within the organisation when needed, to be sure they fully understand its strengths and frailties so they know its potential and the areas needing additional resources.

In summary, a leader must operate on different levels with the fluidity of thinking that allows them to switch mental modes. And more. Having set their goals, a leader must not be dogmatic about the way to reach the goal – good leaders act fast and flexible, they are astute in assessing progress and opportunistic when unforeseen changes arise. All of this is relentless and will at times be mentally and emotionally taxing. A core of resilience is required in leadership.

Sir Richard Carter summed up what is needed as "an ability to see the bigger picture and not take 'no' for an answer in trying to reach your goal. It's never easy in the sense you have to be prepared for setbacks and difficulties that circumstances and people will put in front of you . Circumventing them is part of the major issue in leading your way through to final success.

"Very often there were political difficulties associated with what we wanted to do and those are situations where it's always necessary to circumvent rather than try and go straight through. But again it is hanging onto the longer term view that keeps you going in that direction. It's often much easier to give it all up and walk away, but being able to stick to your guns is, I think, most of the battle."

Leadership, therefore, is often a very personal, internal battle. But one thing is clear. Throughout this process we have referred to the fact no leader can go it truly alone. A leader must have the right team around them.

THE RIGHT STUFF - GETTING THE STRUCTURE RIGHT AND PUTTING THE RIGHT PEOPLE IN THE RIGHT PLACE

Russell Ackoff, the great American management thinker, provides an interesting perspective. In 1979, Ackoff published a seminal paper on organisational research and, in doing so, founded the discipline of Social System Science. He argued the key to business success lay in a focus on interoperability.

Before Ackoff, business metaphors usually referred to an organisation as a mechanism, later refined to be an organism; but his view, typical of a thinker ahead of his time was that each company is a social entity.

Ackoff was trained as an architect to look at a whole building and then move down to the detail. Partly because of this, he saw a company first as a unified whole, then he focused more closely on identifying and dealing with specific lines of tension within the structure.

He provided a simple, perfect summation of business dynamics: "The management of interactions."

Ackoff said managers who had moved from specific line responsibilities and into the realm of general or executive management often needed their greatest focus to be on an overview of the links between the various specialist components of the business. "What he has to do is manage how those specialists interact, *not what they do, but how they do things together* and that is a very different type of management. We are not used to it."

Ackoff was emphasising how the constituent parts of the business pull together to deliver, in a unified way, on the company's goals. Without the ability to work in concert, achievement will be stymied. It's a view of business which places a premium on people.

Good leaders recognise this. "Team" is a word used by all of our business laureates. They praise those around them; modesty, it seems, is also a trait of the best leaders.

Hugh Perrett, typical of a Kiwi businessman, used a rugby analogy to demonstrate this aspect and also highlight that a shrewd leader assesses and understands the talents, and the limitations, of each in the team.

You may have the right person in the team. But critically, you need them in the right place at the right time – for their good, and yours. Business success, Perrett said, is "not one man's effort, it's a question of team, and we had a very good team with a lot of individuals with exceptional talents in different areas.

"In lots of ways, it's not unlike a rugby team where you have 15 players, most of them with different talents and, for example, because a first five-eighth plays exceptionally well, you don't promote him to lock and if you have got an exceptionally good hooker, he doesn't get promoted to halfback. And that, really, is the way that it works: that you harness all these different talents to a common purpose.

"Rugby is a co-ordination of efforts and different talents and skills and really business is very, very similar - in that you have to bring together people of considerably different talents and abilities. You hire them for what they are good at. The [organisational] structure reflects what you need to have to realise your purpose or give effect to your purpose."

It can be argued that the most crucial task for any leader is ensuring the right people are working in the business.

Jim Collins, in *Good to Great*, perhaps best expressed this key tenet of successful business leadership in saying "get the right people on the bus". It's a phrase you will hear often repeated through most businesses these days. As Collins said, there are some simple truths – if you have the right people alongside you, then where the business is headed becomes almost secondary. That's because you can have confidence those around you will change, adapt and focus on success and take you there, no matter where it lies and irrespective of the challenges to be overcome. Secondly, the right people remove much of the burden of management because they are self-motivated and driven. This was a business fact that Sir Roderick Deane knew. "If I have any helpful attributes, they are about choosing great people to work with me (and spending a huge amount of time trying to do this well); being willing to analyse the strategic options thoroughly and being open-minded to the ideas of people who have different intellectual perspectives from my own - I greatly value creativity and imagination and innovation, just as I value the ability to make things happen."

It is instructive to see Sir Roderick acknowledge that a large commitment of his time as a CEO was in considering who to bring on board his bus. And this is because, logically, failing to get the right person will lead you to the wrong one. Perrett: "The worst thing that can happen is that you get someone who doesn't fit the culture: they can be very disruptive; it can cause serious problems inside the business."

And here is Norman on the same issue: "We always make sure that the person fits in, because if they don't fit in, it can absolutely rock the whole boat. You just need one person and it can throw the whole lot

The secret to Ted Lees' success was innovation and one of the keys to sustained innovation is the right team. Lees often personally recruited his team, flying to England to find skilled engineers. He had what might be considered an unusual technique. If he saw a CV he liked, he paid a visit to their home. "I would go out and knock on the door, no warning, and if he is drunk on the couch, we'd turn round and go away, if he's arguing with his wife, we would turn around and go away. One particular guy who ended up here and did very well, I remember him saying: 'Here's all my drawings'. I said: 'Yeah, I've seen those, I want to talk to your wife.' 'What do you want to talk to my wife for?' I said: 'If you come out to New Zealand, you will make friends with the boys at work and you'll go after work and have a beer with them or join a club. But mum's home with the kids, unless she is going to promise me now that she is going to join a church, or join something, or get herself away from just home and kids, I don't want her to come - because in six months they want to go back again, they get so homesick.'" Now these days a mother is as often working as an equal bread winner or engaged in important roles in the community. But Lees, taking a holistic view of the psychology of the entire family unit, was ahead of his time focused on ensuring his staff achieved the right support and work-life balance needed to flourish.

out of kilter. If you don't have a team player it changes the whole dynamic of a store - so you have to get a good balance of talent but also a balance of people who get on with one another."

No matter how good your strategy, your business will never achieve its full potential if held back by poor staff.

A core part of hiring talent is that a leader cannot be an expert in all facets of even the business they themselves have built. Nor should they try. How you compensate for your own lack of skills is precisely the point Jim Collins makes and was echoed succinctly by entrepreneur and business leader Tony Falkenstein: "Hire the right person."

Sir Ron Carter has a thoughtful analysis: "I would describe myself as somebody who recognised the importance of detail. The scale of work that I have been involved in has meant that in most instances I haven't been able to deal with detail myself, but I have been jolly sure I have got somebody who does get the detail right, because the devil is often in the detail and particularly in engineering.

"No one person, certainly not me, but then again no one person within the organisation, has the detail skill necessary to deliver the service, so a lot of my effort, was making sure we brought [that skill] into the firm, we hired people with the skill level necessary and I think our clients expected us to always have somebody who knew the detail of the task they were asking us to do."

Roy Savage provides another example – with an interesting familial flavour. Savage is best known for pioneering workplace safety clothing and equipment companies, with NZ Safety and AlSafe in Australia, while also running the investment vehicle Savage Group Holdings. He saw a need for additional firepower in his top team, to balance his skills, so recruited his own daughter, Catherine Savage, who was then managing director of AMP Capital Investments.

"There's a bit rubbing off both ways," he says. "Catherine is a broad-picture person and I've always been 'crossing the Ts and dotting the Is', and being careful about the administrative details."

How to deal with those you have brought into your team, the specialists, the impact players, and to foster co-operation between them is, of course, a key issue and exactly what Ackoff recognised as one of the core requirements of leadership, that management of interactions.

ESTABLISHING THE RIGHT ENVIRONMENT FOR THOSE RIGHT PEOPLE TO FLOURISH

It is impossible to be prescriptive about the right internal environment for any business to flourish – the cultures of companies can be as varied as their number. Even those that operate within the same sector producing interchangeable products can differ widely. The culture that suits one company and helps propel it to success may be anathema to another. Interestingly, culture may be almost invisible to those embedded within it. John Van Maanen has a nice turn of phrase to express this: "Culture is sort of white space: it's the stuff we breathe." It is only when we see culture violated that we recognise it exists.

Likewise, what motivates individual employees can vary widely. Motivation can be the allure of extrinsic rewards - be it praise, promotion, perks or money - and it can arise from within, the intrinsic satisfaction of fulfilling a personal mission.

But almost universally, people resent any perception they are just cogs in the wheels of business, happy to be kept in ignorance, just completing their allotted tasks for the day. Human beings instinctively want to understand how their work contributes to the whole, whether the overall company is doing well and why.

People desire a sense of belonging – which links back to the Ackoff theory of businesses as social entities. We spoke above about the need to assign stretch goals for individuals, outlining expectations, of setting an overall cracking pace, even at times being unreasonable. This is as it should be. Leaders have a right to be demanding, and even abrasive. But the wise leader also recognises these are human beings he is dealing with – all of us have our fears, our insecurities, our needs, our aspirations.

One further point should be made. No matter what unemployment figures may be doing right now, one of the macro trends of the New Zealand business environment is a workforce shortage, particularly in the area of skilled talent. Too many are wooed offshore by bigger pay packets and brighter lights. It is one of the most limiting factors to growth aspirations that many firms face.

This is why, despite all the differences and variability, one thing is clear. Culture and staff motivation are vital. Tony Falkenstein is one who is certain of this: "If we buy a company getting the culture right is the most important thing before anything else. Getting those people right." All the leaders of the Fairfax Business Hall of Fame emphasise if you have gone to the effort to hire the right person, then you must give those people the right tools and environment to work in – and trust them. It is useful to look at how our leaders achieve the marriage of accountability and discipline with the creativity and trust to allow those right people to flourish.

Some focus on the organisational structure, others on observable culture, others on the need to personally inspire.

Sir Ron Carter: "We have developed, through a process of delegated authority, a very flat business structure in which people have had a lot of opportunity to exercise their own knowledge, but to do so within a framework of control that was set up by the company as a whole."

Sir Wilson Whineray: "You need respect both ways. You can't demand respect. Hopefully you earn respect. They have to feel they are important. You give them responsibility to do jobs, they understand it, they have the skills to do it, they have training. Let them know exactly what you expect, give them what they need and reward them. Get into praise and criticism. Praise should be modest, not fulsome, in public. Criticism should be private. Deal with it on a one on one basis."

Hugh Perrett: "Informality is important; it helps people feel at ease, they are easy about contributing, taking part, feeling they have got something to offer. It also helps cross functional interaction and it avoids to a large extent getting too much of a silo set up. So informality is really about making it easy for people to work together and to contribute."

Tony Falkenstein: "Having that positive attitude is just so important and I think if you go into any of our companies you find there is a buzz, people want to work here. I know the names of everybody on the staff, I think that's important. I have a sheet here of where everyone sits and their names, just to make sure I do know. We have a couple of philosophies – one is if you are not in business for fun and profit, what the hell are you doing here? And we instill that in staff. We say 'hey, if you're not enjoying it here, you're much better off somewhere else', because some people want to work in bureaucracies, for example. We try to make this a fun environment. We have put a lot of effort into having a relaxation room where people can sit in beanbags and watch TVs and do all of that sort of stuff."

Anne Norman: "We have a stockroom. All the staff, it doesn't matter if it is me or the junior, junior, we all pick the stock that is sold that day" to replenish the stock in the stores. "The stock comes up on a picking list, its all bins of diamonds and gold and silver, the number comes up, you pull it out of the bin and scan it and it is packeted up and couriered to the branches. Everybody does it from the CFO to the junior. We are picking the product so the accounts staff understand, this is what we are here for, we buy and sell jewellery, this is the Pascoes' business. And it creates a really good team environment. You pick on a Monday morning, and say 'how did the weekend go', everybody knows what everybody has done. Every day you are next to somebody different, everybody knows one another, everybody understands everybody else's workload better. In Australia at Prouds, the building is about four storeys and one day the accountant died, which was really suddenly. Everybody in the building knew him because they had all picked with him, they had all maybe stood next to him yesterday or the day before. Everybody knew who it was, so whole the building was in mourning, not just people in his department. Sometimes you get a place where people say 'I never even met him, I never knew him.'"

Alan Burnet: "To run a good successful organisation, you have got to have people with you. To start off with, you have got to be fair to all people and above all you have got to set an example and you have got to have integrity. It's no good trying to lead people if they don't think you are the right material and that's the main thing."

Perrett again: "It's largely a matter of your own integrity, your own sense of values and the way you behave yourself. Culture really starts from the top."

The variety of approaches extends even to the changing styles used by individual leaders. Those who have been more conscious of the techniques they employ as leaders show they will readily change their modus operandi as required. Falkenstein: "I haven't got one leadership style. It is like communication, there are two parts [or participants] to it. So I have to be a leader in different ways, depending whom I am leading. Different people require different ways of leading. I look at every situation."

Likening leadership to the transactional communication process is an inspired comparison. Falkenstein's approach also underlines that such theoretical models as situational and contingency leadership are evident in the real world of business, either consciously applied or existing innately within the repertoire of exceptional leaders.

Whatever the differences in approach, there are general parallels that rise to the surface. Each of the leaders interviewed for this book favours creating a 'no-surprises culture'. But to do so, means a no-blame culture. There has to be an acceptance of failure providing it is controlled, flagged and dealt with quickly. Sir Ron Carter has led businesses, been a director of companies and taken Government appointments. Throughout all those tasks, his message for those he delegates tasks to has been consistent – trust and transparency. "The requirement is always the same, let us know how things are going. We expect you to actually be on top of all the matters that have been delegated to you to run, but we also expect you to tell us when things are not going as well as you would like. That gives us the chance to bring the resources of the organisation in to support you."

Sometimes, trusting the right people and giving them the right opportunity to achieve their potential can mean simply getting out of their way.

Perrett: "I didn't like to, and didn't want, to get involved in sticking my nose into everything that everybody did. We had good people and I think you stand back and let them get on with the job, you are there to encourage them, you are there to help coach them if necessary."

None of this runs counter to the recommendation to talk to people within the business to keep yourself informed – the management walk-

Making it Personal

Sir Stephen Tindall provides a good example of a person who moulded his personal drive into a vision to put customers first – similar to the ethical approach highlighted by Dame Wendy Pye. He ensured this vision was at the core of his company culture.

"When I first started The Warehouse, I was really motivated by being able to make a real difference to our customers' lives," he says. "In other words, their standard of living. And once we got through the first stage of survival, which always happens with a start-up, and it became reasonably obvious that we could in fact be quite a big player in the New Zealand context, then the purpose of The Warehouse was very clear: and that was to make the desirable affordable, in other words to give everyone a bargain and at the same time enable them to actually take advantage of the things they needed at lower prices.

"And so we didn't just go to the point where we wanted to be just a little less expensive than our competition, we actually went out and used the efficiencies of supply-chain management and the efficiencies of business to get our costs to a point where we could in fact drive prices way lower. It was this real purpose to make a huge difference to peoples' lives.

"My personal belief is that culture is absolutely paramount, that the difference between a business with a very strong culture and one without is that you have got a 100-year company as opposed to one which may not be around even five years out.

"Ours developed from our very early ethos, which is 'where people come first and quality is affordable'. If you get staff who are highly motivated because they believe in the purpose - to make peoples' lives, your customers lives, a lot easier by having much cheaper prices - then they feel good about what they do. They come to work, they get out of bed every morning thinking: 'I'm actually making a difference, its not just a job, I don't come along just to earn my wages. I come along to actually provide an answer to the purpose.' And I think, as a result of that, we have had very, very motivated staff and that's made a massive difference."

about that Sir Rod Weir champions – it is a matter of degree, balance and intent.

But perhaps none has advocated this approach to such an extreme as Tony Falkenstein. When asked to list his own leadership attributes, he ticked off some standard, obligatory aspects then, intriguingly, added: "The biggest one is just getting out of the business. I suppose recognising 12 years ago 'hey, Tony there are plenty of people who can manage businesses and do it well, and probably even better than you. What you are good at is adding ideas to the business.'

"So in theory I should be sitting on Waikiki beach and just have ideas. And that is what I did. I got out of the business and that is when the business started to grow." Not all have to go to such extremes, of course.

Another common thread, best described by The Warehouse founder Sir Stephen Tindall, was that of conceiving the normal leadership hierarchy as inversed, with the leader as a foundation for the talented staff above. "My leadership style is what's commonly called servant leadership. If you can picture a triangle at the bottom, which would normally be called the apex, you have the leader and then the people that you interface with very carefully at senior management level - the people you are there to support. Their job is to support the next layer up, so that when you are looking at an organisation with a large number of both people and stakeholders the vast majority of those are of course in the thick end of the triangle.

"So I see servant leadership as giving the support, first of all, to the immediate people that would report to you, who in turn do the same up the triangle and therefore you have this very inclusive style. And I think the other thing that I learnt very early in the piece, was the way to really get people's confidence was to show an incredible interest in them. Having them respect you very much for the fact they know you respect them enables you to get probably 100 per cent more out of them, in terms of performance, than you would if they didn't respect you."

Whatever the style a leader uses, the bedrock to leadership is people. And people always respond more fully, engage at a higher degree, if they feel valued and trusted. It is also important that people within a business feel that such trust and respect extends beyond the walls of their company into the wider community. Sir Stephen has said in the past: "Business must be seen as the most important component of making the country tick. Without it, there's no economy. But people don't trust business leaders. The ball is firmly in our court. We've got to earn a social licence to trade." That phrase, social licence, is powerful.

So we have covered the creation and communication of vision and strategy, the need to hire the right people and give them the right support. But Sir Stephen has highlighted one more vital thing a leader needs.

CREDIBILITY

Let's return to where we began, with Dame Wendy Pye.

"Credibility is the most critical issue facing business," she says. Asked for the attributes of leadership, she readily provides the stock answers of strategic vision and disciplined execution. But where she really impresses is in her focus around "taking the troops with you": inspiring loyalty and showing integrity.

These are fundamentals of true business leadership, which encompass staff, customers and peers. To truly succeed in business you must command respect. And you have to earn respect.

Dame Wendy has that in plenty. She has dined with the great and the good, her office is dotted with photos of herself with former US presidents George W Bush and Bill Clinton, she has been part of the Business Roundtable and too many high-powered trade and advisory missions to name. But she has no pomp and circumstance, describing herself as "a very practical housewife" who loves nothing more than gardening and making chutneys.

A large part of what drives Dame Wendy's strong views on business ethics is her passion for her product: she sees her business making a difference to people's lives.

In Dame Wendy's business, such moral high ground might seem easy enough to seize. She produces books for children and what she locks onto is that books teach literacy, create opportunities for people, lift their intellectual horizons. But shouldn't all business be able to focus on the good they are bringing to people? No matter what their product or service, shouldn't there be a kernel of doing what you do because it enriches people's lives. If that notion is your starting point, then integrity is central to your business ethos and your leadership will instinctively reflect it.

Perhaps the most valuable lesson to learn from Dame Wendy is that all businesses should learn moral literacy, which should then be the bedrock of business leadership.

SIR PETER LEITCH: Mad Marketing Genius

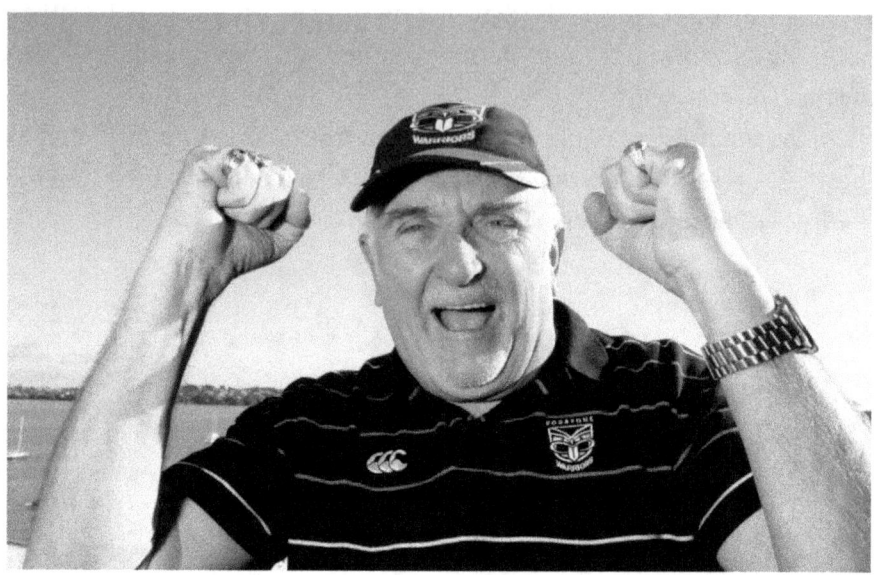

THE Mad Butcher name is just one of many for Peter Leitch. It was bestowed on him by a "young Maori gentleman" who just happened to walk into the South Auckland bar where he and legendary radio man Tim Bickerstaff were discussing a new marketing approach.

The butcher tells the story in his own laconic way. "I was talking to Tim about advertising - he said we needed a gimmick. A young Maori gentleman came in and said, 'There's that f...ing mad butcher' and I said, 'That'll do us'. But Tim said, 'We can't use that F-word but we'll use the Mad Butcher all right'."

As Sir Peter likes to say - the rest is history. That knightly honorific, another of his many names, was bestowed in a slightly more conventional fashion in Queen's Birthday honours, but is no less surprising for the man himself. He is constantly amazed at his own history, at the success that has flown from his life's work. That life of Sir Peter Charles Leitch, QSM, has been well documented in magazines, newspapers and a This Is Your Life television special. For a more in-depth history, he directs punters to his 2008 biography, What a Ride, Mate. But it can be summarised as a life story of hard work, astonishingly so at times for those who are swept up in the whirlwind that is Sir Peter in full swing. That work has built upon an instinctive grasp of marketing, an enviable ease within his own skin which has made him frank, honest, at times brutally so, and – at the heart of it all – an amazing, absolutely authentic, generosity of spirit.

He is a man who benefitted at critical times from others who saw potential in him. And he has always been ready therefore to extend a hand himself, to help.

Co-author of his biography, Phil Gifford, remarked at the launch that the book would have been much longer if he had left all the swear words in. However, for interviews the Mad Butcher, tones his language down. It's a skill that must have taken some adjusting to in the early days of his chain's marketing push, which largely occurred through radio phone-ins. "The success of it was that I got on the radio and made a dick of myself." He says there was no persona - "It was just me, I just done what I done and it worked. I pioneered the phone-ins on radio. I remember I broke the ice on Newstalk ZB; they didn't do live phone-ins but they wanted my business, and I said, 'you don't get my business if I can't do the phone-ins'."

The brand started off as "Rosella Meats - The Home of the Mad Butcher", but was soon persuaded to simplify the title and a marketing legend was born.

"I just rode the wave. It's like a surfer: when you find a good wave you ride it. So I rode the wave of the Mad Butcher and sold the business a few years ago.

"It wasn't an overnight success. It took time and there were some painful moments, some highs and some lows." And at the end of the day, all the acclaim and accolades are, he says "quite an honour for a simple butcher."

The "simple butcher" was very green when he moved to Auckland at 16. He grew up in Newtown, Wellington, as the youngest of seven children. Without a proper diagnosis of his dyslexia, he struggled at school and took work as a telegram delivery boy and then at a butcher's shop in

Seatoun. He eventually made the move north and swapped, as the legend goes, a meat cleaver for a gravedigger's shovel at Purewa Cemetery.

But his ambition for butchery still burned and a job at an Ellerslie meat shop helped him bide time until he could find his vocation - and someone willing to back him.

"I used to go out in my 1950 Morris Minor in the weekend with [daughter] Angela in tow and look at butcher's shops. I looked at a shop in Rosella Rd in Mangere. The owner of the building was a guy called Harold Hill and he ended up financing me into the store. We started there and it was a hard slog."

Hill was managing director of Hancock's Wines and Spirits, a company built by another Business Hall of Fame laureate, Sir Ernest Davis. But, eventually, a new and less-sympathetic landlord meant another change of location, to Massey Rd in Mangere - a shop that still bears the Mad Butcher insignia today.

The empire grew from there and the chain now has 37 locations throughout New Zealand. Although Sir Peter sold the business to his chief executive Michael Morton in 2008, who went on to publically list the company, it was still his mission statement that underpinned the operation.

So what are those values? His daughters Angela and Julie, when asked separately, both espouse the two main pearls of wisdom that he has passed down to them, to his staff and probably to countless footy players: "Treat others as you want to be treated yourself" and "if you're going to do a job, do it properly".

"From day one, Dad has always had a really strong work ethic and we've always known that," Angela says. "Whatever he does he puts 110 per cent into it . . . He's always been a full-steam-ahead kind of bloke.

"He never seems to need the eight hours sleep like I do. He's always got up at 4am and survived on two or three hours sleep. He does a lot. I don't think people realise just how much he does do for charity, where he expects nothing in return, whereas some people get payments."

One friend said the Mad Butcher's honesty is the key to his success.

"It's honesty above all else for him . . . the Mad Butcher persona is not something he puts on. It's who he actually is. Could Pete be the chief executive of Air New Zealand and operate like that? The answer is probably no, because he's a butcher.

"When I grew up in Rotorua you'd be given a chipolata at the butcher's, and the boys would be covered in tattoos with great big knives and wooden chopping boards - they were some pretty down-to-earth people. So Pete's never going to be comfortable heading up Saatchi & Saatchi, but I do think fundamental honesty is a pretty decent business principle."

That honesty extends to the Mad Butcher's marketing approach. He's most proud of the fact he's never been charged for misleading advertising, and if there's one thing that annoys him, its competitors running down his products.

"We're a no-bullshit outfit; we're straight up and down. We call a spade a spade. I never enter into any of this bullshit that other people do. I read a comment the other day by a farmer down in the South Island making sausages saying, 'We don't put rubbish in sausages'.

"Well, I never put rubbish in sausages and I've never slagged off the industry, either. People like that piss me off, to be fair. You don't need to worry about your competition. If you're good just get on with your job."

He's also proud of cutting into the market of his main competition - the supermarkets: "They want to dominate the world. We took them on in our own little way, we ambushed them a little bit and we got a pretty good market share."

As for philanthropy former Fairfax Media journalist David Kemeys says he has witnessed Sir Peter's legendary generosity on many occasions.

They collaborated under the banner of The Mad Butcher - Suburban Newspapers Charitable Trust, which has donated more than $1 million to various causes over seven years. Sir Peter would often ask Kemeys to help distribute his personal cash at charity auctions when the butcher couldn't bring himself to take credit for the donations.

Despite the brash attitude, quick wit and colourful language, it's Sir Peter's humble nature that wins him the most friends and the support of the New Zealand public through his personal health battles – he fought bladder cancer.

Despite all the honorifics and marketing memorabilia, you sense Sir Peter Charles Leitch, QSM, merely wants to be remembered as "a good bloke".

"I had a great friend called Tom Cowley who was a bit of a mentor to me. He worked in the freezing works as a chiller hand. We were at a function one day and I remember him saying to someone, 'I've known the Mad Butcher before he was the Mad Butcher and he's the same bloke today as he was yesterday', and I thought that was a wonderful compliment."

+ Sources for this profile were a one to one interview by William Mace with Sir Peter Leitch and interviews with family and friends.

SIR JOHN PLIMMER: Enterprising Genius

If nothing else Sir John Plimmer was a virtuoso of versatility.

He was a carpenter, a builder, brick manufacturer, land speculator, importer, merchant, landlord, and politician.

And that list is somewhat of an understatement, for a pioneer businessman who transformed both the physical face of Wellington and stamped his personality on the business culture of the capital.

Sir John was one of those exceptional early entrepreneurs who helped create the country's business spirit, setting the platform for the active economic environment we have enjoyed ever since.

He died in 1905 – so what can be learnt from a man who lived a lifetime ago in a New Zealand so different from today? Consider this – are the basic challenges of business so different, is it not about identifying opportunity, having the raw genius to understand how to exploit such openings and having the courage to take a risk along with the communication skills to bring others along with you.

In this Sir John provides a salient lesson in the merits of hard work, vision and taking a calculated punt. So important was his contribution to Wellington that he is known as the 'father of Wellington.'

Descendent, Ian McKinnon, former deputy mayor of Wellington, is reminded daily of the Plimmer legacy to the region he now helps run. "My office is in the town hall and everyday when I walk down the staircase there is a massive portrait of my great, great grandfather. He is rightly known as the father of Wellington."

Sir John was born in 1812 in Shropshire, England, the youngest but one of 12 children of a builder and timber merchant. His parents wanted him to become a teacher but he preferred to follow the family trade and at age 19 became a woodcutter, eventually working as a master builder and plasterer.

Then the advertising of the New Zealand Company, singing the praises of colonising the new land, caught his adventurous spirit. In 1841, after a four and half month trip, Plimmer and young family arrived at Port Nicholson.

Within a week of landing his enterprise and sheer vitality were already apparent. While many new settlers lived in tents for months, Plimmer had built a cabin for his family by the end of that first week . With an earthen floor the cabin was far from the home comforts they were used to in England, but it was, nonetheless, testament to his energy.

Initially he worked within the trade he knew, earning money felling timber, cutting posts and rails, and did some building work. But that entrepreneurial spirit soon saw him branch out. Instead of selling all the timber he began to burn charcoal and then set up a small lime works and moved into manufacturing his own bricks. He began building brick houses for other new settlers using his own lime and bricks.

He prospered and built two more houses for his own family. One was famed for a wooden dove above the door, which his descendants are said to still own; the other was a fine brick building which later became the famed Barrett's Hotel on the corner of Lambton Quay and Willis St. All was going well until successive earthquakes in 1848 and 1855 discouraged building in brick and brought wooden houses back in favour. Proving his flexibility, Plimmer readily switched back to his first trade as a carpenter and continued constructing wooden houses for the growing town, as well as repairing buildings damaged by the earthquakes.

It was while working around Lambton Quay that Plimmer realised the importance of wharves for the growing town and, in typically bold fashion, decided to extend himself from simple building into property development – he would build himself a wharf. The way he went about it also highlights the hall mark of entrepreneurial success – the ingenuity of adapting to opportunity. An American ship Inconstant had foundered off Pencarrow Head. Plimmer bought the wreck and had it towed to the foreshore near Lambton Quay on what is now known as the old Bank of New Zealand site where he turned it into a makeshift private wharf, business office and bonded warehouse.

Quickly nicknamed Plimmer's Ark because of its strange resemblance to the biblical Noah's Ark it proved highly profitable and was in use for 20 years until 1883. In 1998 remaining pieces of the boat were discovered and excavated during building work on the site.

While enjoying the profits of his impromptu wharf making, Sir John also busied himself pushing along reclamation work and improved port facilities. These contributed greatly to Wellington's emergence from a provincial backwater to an economic centre in its own right.

He measured the distance from Cuba St to Pipitea Point, calculated the financial results of the reclamation and then convinced Governor Sir George Grey to approve the work for the betterment of wider Wellington.

Sir John's entrepreneurial skills did not initially endear him to local merchants but the profits from the wharf venture enabled him to invest in the local economy, not least hotels. He built or managed many notable Wellington hotels, including the Albert Hotel, the City Hotel, and a hotel on the Tramways site in Newtown.

He was a founding member of the Wellington Chamber of Commerce and, showing his hand at marketing and communication, began writing in local newspapers. He promoted the development of the province – it helped that he was a director of the New Zealand Times newspaper.

Incidentally, he was twice married, first in England to Mary Roden who sailed out with him to New Zealand and after her death to Janet Anderson, a sister of John Anderson, editor of the Wellington Independent newspaper.

The most important of his investments was the Wellington & Manawatu Railway Company, which he helped promote and on whose board he served until 1900.

Plimmer was the shareholder who moved the first resolution pledging the company to construct the rail line from Wellington to Manawatu which greatly reduced the costs of freight at a time of economic recession. The company became New Zealand's most successful private railway venture and the rail line was probably his greatest legacy to the development of Wellington.

He was also active in local politics – which he used as a platform to again push for better business and civic conditions. He was elected to the Wellington Provincial Council in 1857, using his influence to get a bill passed to vest in the town its remaining reserves.

Then after successfully organising a ratepayers' petition to the Government to make Wellington a city, he was one of the first councillors to serve on the new Wellington City Council, formed in 1870. His descendants also made significant contributions to Wellington's economy, including a grandson, William Harcus Plimmer (1874–1959), who was the musical and dramatic critic on the Dominion newspaper for many years. His great-grandson Sir Clifford Plimmer was head of Wrightsons and was himself inducted posthumously into the Business Hall of Fame in 1995. Sir John also had four distinguished great, great grandchildren, the brothers McKinnon — Ian the deputy mayor of Wellington and pro-chancellor of Victoria University, Sir Donald former Foreign Minister and Commonwealth Secretary-General, John the secretary of Defence and Malcolm a prominent historian.

+ Sources for this profile include business journalist and historian Graeme Hunt, the Museum of Wellington and work by Bernard Foster in the Encyclopaedia of New Zealand and interviews by David Gadd with the Plimmer family.

ABOVE ALL ELSE - KNOW THYSELF

Few people dare to stare down media magnate Rupert Murdoch – and even fewer pull it off. But Alan Burnet did.

It's testimony to the personal courage and deal-making skills that were Burnet's hallmark as he built New Zealand's most significant media company. It was Burnet who swung the series of acquisitions to create Independent News Limited, which became part of Murdoch's global media empire. It was ultimately sold in 2003 to Australian-owned company Fairfax Media, which has published this material.

Murdoch is a man Burnet knows well, and describes as "an extraordinary fellow" of enormous energy, "vital, quick and unconventional".

"He is a person who can have immense charm, and can be an absolute bastard," Burnet adds.

The two men fell out when Burnet stitched together a deal to bring another daily newspaper into the Murdoch fold, as Burnet puts it, "pinched from under the noses" of their rivals. The complex deal required the issuing of fresh shares, which watered down Murdoch's stake in his New Zealand holdings, something which displeased the magnate. Burnet, politely, says Murdoch "got grumpy" with him: "I was well aware he could have fired me." Here's the key: Burnet backed himself, and his own reputation. Refusing to give in, he knew the deal he had structured was the best possible, regardless of what Murdoch said. After a tense time, Murdoch eventually backed down - ultimately, acknowledging Burnet had negotiated a good deal. Indeed, he later paid Burnet a significant compliment, considering Murdoch's relentless oversight of his company's performance. When Burnet chided him for not visiting New Zealand more often, the reply was: "Why do I need to come when you are doing so well?"

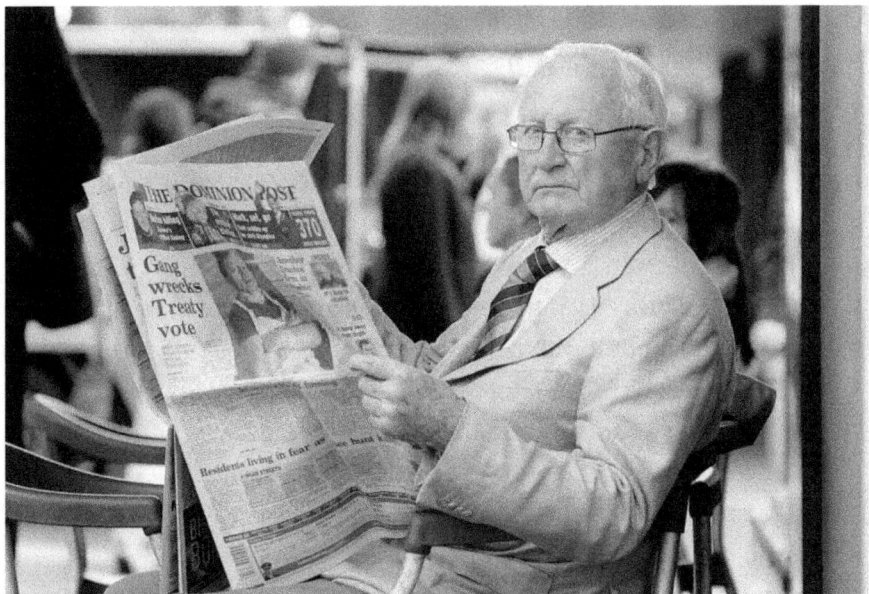

Alan Burnet

In this moment of personal pressure where others might have buckled, Burnet exemplified what was identified in the Chapter the *Zen of Management* as the single most important piece of advice from all the leaders who have contributed to this book: Know thyself.

If you step into a leadership role, whether in the corporate role or in building your own business, you will work immensely long hours, sometimes at the expense of family and the things you treasure. The oft-cited work-life balance can be hardest to find at the top. You will face failure, you will face stress, but fortitude comes from the inner certainty that what you're doing is right and worth it.

There will come times however when everything is put on the line – both your business and your personal career, everything you've built and everything you plan and most importantly, your own sense of worth and your values. You confront all of this when you decide whether you want to be, and whether you should be, the leader.

This isn't a textbook on motivation or a self-help guide. Everyone has to decide whether they have what it takes, and if they possess the appetite to become a leader. The foundation of this book is to give you an unparalleled access to the thinking and life-lessons of the achievers in the Business Hall of Fame. This chapter offers an insight into the forces and personality traits that have propelled them to the top and the key characteristics they possess.

Perhaps more than anyone else to contribute to this book, Sir Rod Weir took us directly into the very personal, talking frankly about what caused the great sense of responsibility that drove him to success. At the age of just 40, his father suffered complications associated with jaundice. It's a condition that would today be easily dealt with – but in 1941 left him lying in a hospital bed slipping inexorably towards death.

"I remember going to the hospital one day to see him and he said to me, 'I'm going to die, you are the eldest in the family, you look after the family,' " says Sir Rod. "It was a stupid thing to say to a 12-year-old boy. But he did say it. And in a week he did die.

"I thought of my mother, and I have a younger brother and [his two-month-old] baby sister. I thought, 'well, there must be a way to get to look after them and make sure we've got security for the future'.

"I was going to do something to try to get some assets together to look after the family and myself. So that was a terrifically motivating thing for me. I think to some extent it was a fear of being poor. I left school on my fifteenth birthday and joined the firm at 19 shillings a week and started work on the third of August; my birthday is 14 July, so two weeks later I started work."

Sir Rod's example of committed hard work clearly paid off. His baby sister would grow up to become the acclaimed concert organist Dame Gillian Weir. Sir Rod's story is also evidence you can start on the bottom rung, and against the odds, make it to the very top of the ladder. Amongst the laureates, there are those who are the scions of a dynasty and have started life with considerable backing. But for each who was blessed by fortune there is a Peter Leitch – a dyslexic former grave-digger – or a Rod Weir, who built their own wealth through brains, personality, and hard work.

Sir Rod's story may be exceptional, but the distinctive dynamics of each family inevitably contribute strongly to the blueprint of our personalities. Ted Lees, for instance, identified sibling rivalry playing a key role in forging his determination to succeed. "As a younger brother I had to prove I could contribute to the business," he said.

The experiences of Lees and Sir Rod were different, but for both, they created a resolve that only increased with hard work, another common element: natural talent may be present, but so is significant graft to hone those skills.

Sir Rod also touched on another of the elements that contribute to leadership — fear. It is perhaps an unlikely element, and this is no attempt at pop psychology, but undeniably these are people who set themselves high standards, and while they don't like failure, they accept it happens; and, perhaps, fear it.

Sir Graeme Douglas, who built his $145 million turnover Douglas Pharmaceuticals from the ground up through unceasing effort, is one who talks of a combination of personal ego, appetite for risk and the ever present perils of failure that drove him. "Once you start, and its not always realised by the general community, once you start a business you normally go into debt and that itself is a driver, particularly so if you have got a mortgage that is at risk. You've also got your own reputation at risk. So quite apart from just wanting to make it a success in an egotistical manner there is that driver of 'gracious, if I don't make a success of this there is going to be some serious embarrassment for me personally and potentially for my family and my colleagues.' So they are very pertinent drivers - just the fact that you have put yourself at risk and you wish to remove that risk as quickly as possible. I guess any business puts itself at risk when it tries innovation, when it enters a market place, because there are obviously always others who want a slice of what you want.

"Many people certainly would not do it and I can seriously understand that because you've got to be prepared, certainly in the formative times of your business, to throw away any concept of a 40 hour week, a 9-5 Monday to Friday. That goes. It goes very quickly. And you will find that most successful businessmen anywhere who start from scratch, and that's certainly my particularly position, then you have just got to give it your best shot and there is just not time let alone the personal energy, frankly, to give to anything else until you get sufficiently established so that finally there is some credit in the bank and you have got some good people with you who share your ambitions. I really can understand why a lot of people would look at what you have to sacrifice and think no that's not for me."

And there is no letting up at the top, in Sir Graeme's view. While that initial drive to stave off personal financial ruin may pass, it is replaced by the ceaseless drive to keep growing the position of yourself and your company.

"Unless you keep a business growing and interesting then you are certainly not going to keep, let alone attract, the good people who can keep it growing and interesting. It is one of those wheels you hop on and it is not that easy to hop off. There is no 'we'll just stay as we are', that's untenable for all sorts of reasons, not least your own personal ego. But that goes through to your client base too, they want new products or new innovations of old products and they want top class service, all of those ingredients that make commerce work. If you are going to play any part then you've got to keep growing your business. And that is I guess the number one driver of a lot of us in commerce, you have just got to keep at the wheel."

Sir Ron Carter takes up this theme: "I've always been very conscious that I've been working in a service industry, it's an industry built upon providing a service to other people that they have requested.

"Once somebody shows that level of confidence in me, then I am really determined to not let them down. It would be too strong a word to say fear of failure has driven me, but determination to make sure I have got it right is certainly something I have paid a lot of attention to. It is very, very important to me not to be wrong. I've always seen myself as trying to make other people's businesses succeed."

That last passage is important – contributing to the success of others. It is a theme you can see in what Sir Rod Weir has said, it exists in Ted Lees' philosophies and you will detect it within the thoughts of every other leader in this book – these leaders are not one-dimensional egos intent on their own success, they are service-oriented. They work to build a legacy to hand on to family, a company to endure which will give surety to a workforce that depends on them and confidence to shareholders. There are often immense philanthropic deeds which flow from these people – look at the examples of Marianne Caughey-Smith-Preston, Douglas Goodfellow and John Ilott. It has to be this way, because these leaders are passionate about what they do.

As Anne Norman comments: "You are not going to be satisfied for long if you are not doing something you enjoy doing. It makes a difference."

Hugh Perrett illustrates this: "First of all, unquestionably for leadership of a business, you need to have integrity and I think integrity embraces honesty and sincerity, it embraces morality and it embraces ethics.

"I'd say you need to have passion for the business, and for its purposes and its vision. You have to strongly, emotionally identify with those things. And that's what passion is about. You may be ambitious, but it's the drive and achievement which needs to be aimed at the business rather than yourself. You need to have a good level of energy because you obviously have to make things happen, often you operate under considerable amounts of stress, you might be faced with long and perhaps arduous hours and all of those things are energy-draining."

That passion, combined with an undeniably iron will, is what drives leaders onwards to success despite all the hurdles and the effort required. Indeed, with some leaders there is almost a need to seek out success in whatever they do, an unrelenting will to keep challenging themselves. Earlier in this book we discussed Sir Wilson Whineray's thoughts on the need for confidence and his own competitive streak – remember this is a man who has had incredible success both on the sports field and in business. So it is worth returning to his views in more depth. He draws an interesting argument of how the two, confidence and competition, are intertwined and feed on each other in a virtuous spiral of self-fulfilment. He advises to seek out challenges: "I've always been somewhat competitive by nature and what interests me with any job I've been given is to try and do it well.

"It is very embarrassing to be given a task, and fail at it or mess it up. So it is not a matter of a financial reward, more the pleasure of feeling you have done something well. And of course once you start doing that, you develop a confidence that almost in the back of the mind is the little voice saying 'give me a tough job and I will handle it'. You don't run

Sir Wilson Whineray

away from the jobs.

"I can remember on my last day of business school the professor there wasn't many years older than I was, because I was in my early 30s when I went, and he said 'I will give you some advice, fellows and girls. Get a job when you leave here where you can be measured. If you are in sales or marketing, where there are sales or marketing results quarterly or annually or semi-annually, production measured on output or wastage or goods per hour, goods per unit of energy used and so on. Financial measures as well. Then you can build up a feeling of success, that you have done something tough and you've done it well.' He said then you can carry on and build on that. I didn't understand what he was saying at the time, I don't think, but I certainly do now. So my motivation was always trying to do something well, and it was the same in sport.

"Some people are born competitive. All of us remember kids in the class at school who were always in the front of the queue or the tuck shop line, first one out with the ball. I think you are born that way, but you can change as you go along.

"And it doesn't mean that you have got a real level of confidence at 24 or 25 or 26 – because you haven't, you haven't faced the challenges then. As you go up [the business hierarchy] you are getting tougher and tougher jobs to do, more demanding and more measurable."

And that, according to Sir Wilson Whineray, is what builds confidence. Find a challenge, nail it, feel the flow of confidence that will set you up to tackle the next and bigger challenge.

"One of the most wonderful things that we can develop in our children and others is confidence – that they can handle what comes up," he says. "Part of it is education, part of it is just doing things well, part of it is succeeding at something. It doesn't matter what it is – it can be a sporting thing, it can be art, music, dance, growing a decent garden. You have just got to do something well and think 'I can do things well'."

Tony Falkenstein is another who believes a person can reach inside and transform themselves. To confidence and competitiveness, he adds a third quality, creativity.

"I have this theory, which academics don't agree with, that entrepreneurs can be made," he explains. "When we are at pre-school, we are all very creative and if we have a ruler, we can turn that into a rocket ship or a sword or a road, anything we like, we can do anything. Then because we do 12 years of schooling where you are dealing with facts, you lose that sense of creativity. The bright kids are the ones who can put facts together. And the dumb kids are the ones who can't. But I think that entrepreneurship is creativity plus execution."

Execution, he says, can be learned, but creativity is innate, so each of us needs to remember the child we once were and rekindle that creative spark.

Anne Norman adds one further and important element to the mix. Business is so often seen as a man's world, and the overwhelming number of laureates in the Business Hall of Fame are men, yet Norman holds her own in any business grouping. And her gender has been far from a hindrance, she says. "I have been lucky being a female, it has been a real advantage. I think women are probably more direct - men will beat around the bush the bit. I remember being in a room full of bankers and we were talking about something and a banker said 'look I might be conflicted here, do you think I should leave the room?'

Nobody said a word until I said 'well yes, I think you should.' The men didn't want to offend the other man, whereas being the only female there, I could. They all felt a bit embarrassed to tell one of their colleagues that he should leave the room." It is an important reminder, pertinent to everyone regardless of gender – to remember we all have inherent limitations and no matter how driven, self assured or confident we may be, it is always good advice to consider the strengths, the merits, the contributions others can provide.

Drive, determination, willpower, passion, integrity, service to others, confidence, competition and creativity: all powerful concepts to live by. Ultimately though, there is one more word to add to the list of those personal traits you will find in our leaders. No matter how hard it may be, no matter the stresses and strains, ultimately the reward must outweigh the effort. The reward in building yourself and your business must lie inside you - and you have to *enjoy* it.

Last words from Tony Falkenstein: "I enjoy this, I enjoy working. I enjoy seeing people being successful." And that's how it should be.

SIR PATRICK HIGGINS: Building a business

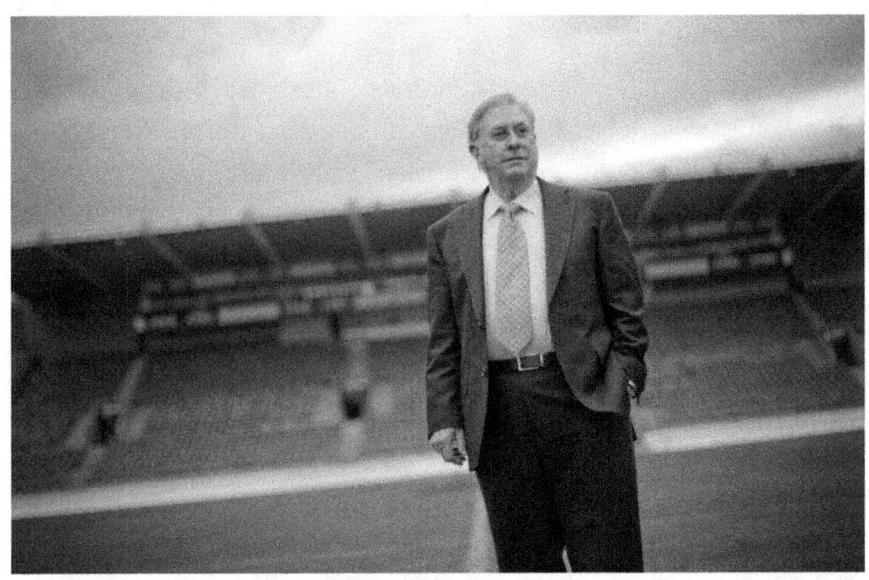

The fumes billowing off the freshly sprayed asphalt catch at the back of the throat. Sir Patrick Higgins doesn't seem to notice, nor apparently care that the smoke might taint his smart suit. He could just be in splatter range, too.

A Higgins roading construction crew is traversing Churcher St outside Feilding High School. Sir Patrick, who is still getting used to being addressed as a knight, is explaining the resealing process.

Then the truck spraying the bitumen stops just metres from where the boss is standing. The driver leaps out onto the freshly laid road and heads straight for Sir Patrick, his hand extended. "Gidday, Pat."

"Gidday, Bobby. How's it going?" the Higgins Group chairman grins.

The penny drops. This is why Manawatu embraces this man. Sir Patrick is an ordinary bloke who has done extraordinary things for a region he and his family love dearly.

He shares a little story about the truck driver. Bobby Cooper is the son of Wally, who has served the company almost from its inception in

1958. At the time, Sir Patrick and his late father, Dan, who co- founded D Higgins and Son, had one fulltimer - their first employee. When he left in 1961, Wally Cooper took the job. Sir Patrick chuckles as he finishes the tale: Wally's grandson now also works for the company. "We call him Mini Cooper."

Sir Patrick, 73 at the time of this interview, has always loved machines and a family history book shows him driving a tractor at the age of 9. When he was 12 he began driving excavators on drainage or construction sites, where he spent many school holidays following his father.

"I've come from very, very basic equipment, some of it made after World War II, locally," he says. The young company had to make many of its own parts. "Fortunately Dad was an A-grade mechanic and very keen on machinery which is obviously where I caught on. It was difficult. There wasn't the work around or the guarantee or continuity of business."

Father and son endured, with considerable help from his late mother, Phyllis. But history could have plotted quite a different course. Today, Sir Patrick might have been a farmer. In 1926 his father was just 19 and had his heart set on working his own land in New Zealand.

Dan Higgins left his home in County Down in Ireland and initially found work on farms but the Great Depression put paid to him owning a slice of paradise for himself. He took on any work he could find and eventually found employment with British Pavements in Christchurch, where he came to excel in roading and drain- laying.

He took those skills to Palmerston North when the company expanded in 1947 and in the mid-1950s set up his own drainage and road repair business in loose partnership with others. Higgins was created in 1958 when Sir Patrick joined his father.

"Dan wasn't so interested in the business side of things. Mother was quite a dynamo and I suppose I may have inherited some of that, " Sir Patrick says. "Phyllis looked after administration and Dan and I were out on site."

The main thrust in the early years was major pipe- laying jobs in the city. "There was a resurgence in a lot of infrastructure work throughout the country. We managed to take advantage of that and do reasonably well at it. We reinvested whatever we made after paying horrendous tax - in those days it was probably 66 cents in the dollar."

They could see the growth potential in maintenance-type work and used Dan's expertise with bitumen projects to take the company forward into road maintenance and construction.

Higgins later became more of a family affair. Sir Patrick's brothers, Michael and Bernard, joined in the 1960s and 1970s. These two decades were a time of rapid expansion as Higgins grew into the areas of civil construction, and the manufacture and supply of aggregates, concrete and bitumen. In addition, Higgins developed expertise in pavement construction, spray sealing, asphalt paving and drainage.

"Work was still confined to the Manawatu, then we quietly expanded from there, mostly by acquisition early on, and we would take opportunities with gravel supply situations to set up our quarries, " Sir Patrick says. "We felt that that was the way to go and also gave us that competitive advantage."

Many of their plans regarding acquisition opportunities would be worked through rather informally. "The strategic plan would take about 10 minutes over a cup of tea. We were really hitting our straps in the mid-70s . . . Bernard, myself and Michael were nicknamed The Front Row.

"We all had different attributes and, being a typical Irish family, I was the oldest and so I was the boss - so I presume I was the man in the middle inside the props."

Higgins has been at the forefront of building New Zealand's infrastructure and today is one of the leading roading construction and civil contracting specialists in the country. Its support office is still in Palmerston North and it has 1200 staff throughout the North Island and upper South Island, specialising in civil contracting, concrete, bitumen, asphalt and aggregate manufacture and supply.

He will not divulge company turnover but says it is "substantial".

Sir Patrick, who shuns the limelight, was rendered almost speechless after he was knighted in 2010 for services to philanthropy and the community.

"I'm feeling very, very humble and surprised, " he told the Manawatu Standard newspaper at the time. "You sort of have difficulty believing it because you never, ever think that you're going to get any honour like this. I've never done anything, thinking of getting honoured for it."

The citation noted his support for community groups including Arohanui Hospice, Manawatu Cancer Society and the Louise Perkins Foundation, and sporting pursuits, including the Manawatu Turbos and Mansfield Park.

He and his wife, Kay, have contributed heavily to the Manawatu Rugby Academy which nurtures strong talent. All Black Aaron Cruden has been among the recipients.

These days, Sir Patrick is attempting to wind down and has, with brother Bernard, gone over succession plans. Bernard, the group's managing director, will take over as chairman.

He, meanwhile, doesn't spend much time out in the field. "But I'm in the office two or three hours a day and then I have these other activities - private investments that I look after on behalf of our families - and that keeps me well occupied at the moment."

+ *Sources for this profile were a one to one interview by Nick Krause with Sir Pat Higgins*

SIR JOHN TODD: Family Philanthropy

Making money is not a sin, but if you are successful you have a moral responsibility to help others.

This according to Sir John Todd, who for many years headed Todd Corporation, one of New Zealand's largest companies, estimated to be worth anything from $2.7 billion to $4 billion. The business revolves largely around the energy sector – an industry that requires leaders with a high appetite for risk because of the need to sink money into projects with no guarantee of return.

Most often the public perception of the oil industry is with large multinational, faceless corporations that dominate the sector. The Todd Corporation though is firmly a family business and Sir John was steeped within the ethos of a dynasty that built the company over the years. At the same time he also headed the expansive family and its wider interests. This fusion of family values and big business is an interesting case to consider and provides a connection back to the profile of Marianne Caughey Smith Preston and the theory of Columbia University economics professor Jagdish Bhagwati whose argument is that capitalism flourishes when the rich spend their money to help others.

The family ensures it is highly visible in passing many of the gains of the business back to the community. The 200-odd members of the Todd family give away millions each year through their family foundation to groups working with children, families, science and the environment.

"We've had success in making money and some people think that's a sin. Making money is not sinful, as long as you are not riding roughshod over anybody else. If you make money, there is a degree of moral responsibility to society to do what you can to help society in a reasonable way."

The Todd Foundation was set up to provide money to a wider range of groups who needed help, rather than helping out in a "personal and private way", which could be ad hoc.

This accumulation of wealth arose from what Sir John calls the "fluke" of hitting gas first time at the Kapuni field in Taranaki. Its interests now include natural gas, oil, LPG, electricity, cogeneration and even solar hot water systems. Outside of the energy industry it also has interests in property, Winemakers, a healthcare company, a large stake in Sky TV, and a big investment in an Australian firm.

Sir John started out in the family firm at 18, spot-welding cars at Todd Motors in Petone. He has worked throughout the business, on the car assembly lines, as an office boy, in spare parts, warehousing, in the office and selling cars. He progressed upwards and in 1987 took over as chairman from the late Sir Bryan Todd, his uncle. But it was not necessarily a role he wanted.

"It was thrust on me - the responsibility to be the head of the family and business. I said, 'well, go for it . . . but it was certainly a major crisis in my life.'"

He nethertheless became part of an illustrious family tradition stretching back to his grandfather Charles who started the original business in the 1880s. Charles, had a reputation as a strong business manager though Sir John only knew him when he was a young teenager, and recalls him as a kindly old man. "He was the origin of so much of our success and his sons inherited his acumen."

The family business started in the South Island town of Heriot in 1885. Todd's great grandfather had been a gold mine manager in Australia, but decided to come to New Zealand, backing his son into business at age 18.

At first it was a wool scouring business, later becoming a stock and station business and then moved into cars, with a sub- dealership for Ford cars in Otago. What follows is an interesting pattern of the opportunistic launching of a business, only for the successful enterprise to fail in the face of external issues. Yet what underlies this is critical – an adaptive, energetic refusal to simply come to a halt, instead there are deft leaps into conjunctive industry sectors. It is a salient lesson in controlled and logical diversification.

Charles' son, Sir Desmond Todd, even as a teenager aimed to expand the car business throughout New Zealand. The first car they sold was a Gray and a dealer organisation was set up around the country. "My father was so successful he sold 400 Gray cars in one year - it was a big number for those days." Todd Motors' success caught the attention of Chrysler and it gained that as the first major franchise in 1925. In the 1930s government regulations imposed a duty on imported cars, which made it "very desirable" to assemble cars in New Zealand.

From 1935 Todd's Petone plant in Wellington put together Chryslers, Hillman and Humbers. In the 1960s Todd Motors bought a large piece of land in Porirua and built a plant with the capacity to make up to 20,000 cars and trucks a year.

"That was a major project and I was managing director of the company at that time," Sir John says.

The first vehicles came off the line in 1972. But protective tariffs were cut over the years and eventually the Porirua plant could no longer compete with cars made in Japan. Overseas manufacturers dominated, selling at a price that left Todd no profit margin. Todd Motors was sold to Mitsubishi in 1987.

As a natural fit with a motor vehicle maker, the Todd Corporation had also been involved in importing petrol – and here too, international events severely impacted the business, with the early 1970s oil crisis meaning its partner refused to renew its supply contract.

"It was imperative to move out of the business - the business would have gone broke if we had to buy on a world retail market for New Zealand," Sir John said. So here also a major part of the business was sold off.

But, as ever, there were new strategies. The company had also moved into the upstream petroleum business of exploration. It was led by Bryan Todd and the company reviewed the government geological records and history of oil exploration. With new techniques they thought it was possible to try drilling again for oil in New Zealand, after earlier attempts in the 1930s.

"Nobody else was interested in New Zealand, so we applied for a lot of [exploration] areas in New Zealand and they gave them all to us," Sir John says.

But deep drilling in Taranaki was beyond Todd's own financial resources. Shell was invited in and took 75 per cent of the share in the area around Kapuni, with Todd down to a quarter. Shell paid for the drilling work. Under an international "knock for knock" agreement, BP came in too, taking half of Shell's 75 per cent. Shell BP Todd was formed to drill Kapuni.

"By sheer good luck the first well which was drilled struck natural gas - it was a fluke - in oil exploration you are lucky to get one well in 10, " Sir John says.

"For us to hit the first one gave us a great deal of strength of resolve to carry on, because we could not finance exploration activity over the years. We could see there was gas there and that gave us enough encouragement to carry on. Todd Energy would not have its position today, if it were not for the fact we started off with 25 per cent of Kapuni."

Later, BP sold out to Todd which now holds half of the gas field. Currently, Todd has about 20 different exploration activities around Taranaki.

When he ran the energy business, Sir John said his basic philosophy was to protect the environment. "I'm also in favour of protecting the rights of individual factions. I'm a liberal. But I believe some of the factions looking after individual interest, whatever they might be . . . try to exert too much influence beyond what is necessary or desirable."

For instance, he was critical of protests in recent years against oil exploration on the East Coast. "They are over-exerting their views. Why should they stop other people doing something which can be of value, to their own interests and New Zealand's interests?"

In his 80s he began to wind down, eventually stepping aside as chair, though he still retains an office in the Todd building from which to do his philanthropic and trustee work, but he has no other specific plans for retirement.

+ Sources for this profile were a one to one interview by James Weir with Sir John Todd

PHILANTHROPY AND SOCIAL ENTREPRENEURSHIP

The lure of gold has attracted many a man, and so it was with Thomas George Macarthy who left London to carve out a life in the pioneer goldfields of first Victoria, Australia, then Otago and onto the West Coast. But he found his fortune when he gave up panning for gold, instead realising an even more lucrative opportunity supplying liquid gold to all those other thirsty gold hunters. He set up a brewery.

His first foray was in 1867 in the tiny gold field frontier town of Charleston, just south of Westport on the coast. From there it was not long before his canny business sense reaped bigger rewards. Rather than digging himself, he was able to able make investments in mines and from there he expanded. Within a decade he had relocated to Wellington and bought into more breweries, cemented himself as an establishment figure with interests in the railway company, the building of an opera house, on the board of the Bank of New Zealand, president of the Wellington Racing Club, and owning hotels, city and suburban homes, valuable business blocks in prime city locations and a sizeable share portfolio in a raft of companies.

At the time of his death in 1912 he left behind an estate of £500,000 (roughly converted to $88 million 100 years later). . His life is packed with lessons of entrepreneurship, that all important combination of calculated risk and opportunism. But it is his death that is actually even more illustrative.

When TG Macarthy died he left half of his immense fortune in a charitable trust to provide for the greater good of his fellow Wellingtonians. And when his wife died childless in 1934, the rest of the estate also joined the trust. In one act, Macarthy became the "father of philanthropy" in New Zealand.

Not only is the trust he created the longest-running of the 470 perpetual charitable trusts the Public Trust operates, it is also possibly the largest. On average, the trust distributes $2m to $3m a year and by

2012 it had distributed $58.6 for "charitable and educational purposes." All registered schools, kindergartens, play centres, kohanga reo, Pacific Island language groups and Plunket organisations in the bounds of the old Wellington province receive donations on a biennial or annual basis by right, without the need to even submit applications. Other groups to benefit are organisations which help children and young people develop and realise their potential; those that look after and provide care and dignity for older people; those that improve the quality of life for the disadvantaged and marginalised; and those that provide essential medical and emergency services. At a High Tea reception held at Government House in Wellington to mark the founding of his trust, more than 123 organisations that have received grants from the TG Macarthy Trust attended.

The board which governs the trust is a roll call of the good and the great – headed by the Governor-General and including the Wellington Mayor, the Roman Catholic Archbishop of Wellington and a former cabinet minister acting as the Prime Minister's representative. "As trustee, we feel privileged to administer this Trust. It's wonderful to see the positive impact Thomas George Macarthy continues to have on people throughout the region," Public Trust Chief Executive Grenville Gaskell said. All this, based on the generousity of a man, son of a Catholic florist father and a Quaker mother, who left his home half a world away to chance his luck.

During his life he had always contributed to good causes, but he had done so anonymously. In his obituary he was described as being a very quiet, reserved man who never courted publicity. "He was, however, of a kindly nature and ever ready to give unostentatiously in the cause of genuine charity."

At the awards ceremony that saw Macarthy inducted as a laureate posthumously into the Business Hall of Fame, Governor General Jerry Mataparae paid this tribute. "These awards promote things that are important to New Zealanders. They honour people whose lives speak of passion - for enterprise, for excellence, for people and for their communities. Tonight we celebrate real-life people who put a face to the ideas and notions behind entrepreneurship, enterprise and hard work. Tonight we celebrate their achievements and their service to New Zealand. As we deal with our current economic difficulties, their lives serve as inspirational exemplars of success."

It picks up an important point. Macarthy is hailed as the father of philanthropy but he is not alone, his example has inspired others and engrained a spirit of philanthropy into New Zealand's business community.

But such philanthropy is not without debate. Should a business leader engage in trying to achieve social good?

Ardent adherents of the likes of Milton Friedman argue capitalism must not be restrained, that pursuit of profit is the only ethically defensible position for business and it is through generating economic growth alone that meaningful social improvement can be attained.

They are countered by those who say that morally bankrupt businesses have no future with cynical consumers, that we must embrace greater involvement in social outcomes.

Bill Gates, the greatest philanthropist of modern times in dollar terms, having established a US$30 billion charitable foundation, stirred emotions with his controversial 2008 Davos speech in which he promoted 'creative capitalism' - where the vital, self serving vigour of capitalism is somehow fused with social goals.

Esteemed Columbia University economics professor and special adviser to the UN and WTO, Jagdish Bhagwati has said capitalism flourishes and its dynamism is enhanced if the pursuit of wealth is balanced with public philanthropy - "if the rich spend their money not on themselves but on social projects."

This has been the pattern throughout history of all successful flowerings of capitalist economic growth, he says. Corporate social responsibility is a necessary modern counterpart of the long standing traditions of "wonderful family-owned businesses."

You need only read through the biographies of the laureates, gathered here in this work, to understand how much they have driven NZ forward, not just economically, but socially, through just such enormous philanthropic endeavors that Bhagwati champions.

If we go back to the legacy Macarthy created in New Zealand business, we see the list is long of those laureates who followed his path and established charitable trusts and foundations. In doing so, they gave their philanthropic endeavours a permanence beyond just the donations they all personally made during their lifetimes. It is worth listing at least some of them, just to emphasise how lengthy the roll call is. Two years after Macarthy died and left his first bequest, in 1915 shipping magnate and investor Thomas Cawthron similarly made an extensive bequest, of £231,000 (in modern day terms $30-$40 million), to set up the Cawthron Institute. It is now New Zealand's largest independent and not-for-profit scientific research organisation. A decade later, in 1927, Sir Percy Sargood, head of a sprawling Dunedin-based commercial import and manufacturing business, gifted the bulk of his estate as a trust fund for the benefit of the arts, youth and education. His bequest followed a lifetime of good deeds and support of community initiatives. During her lifetime self-made businesswoman Marianne Caughey Smith Preston gifted property to the then Auckland Hospital Board for a convalescent home for women and children, other property to the Methodist Church for an orphanage and numerous pieces of park land to Auckland city. At her death, her will bequeathed her shareholding in the Smith & Caughey department store to set up a rest home which continues to operate today.

Other laureates didn't wait to leave bequests, they created charitable trusts during their lifetimes. In 1938 retailer Sir John McKenzie founded the J R McKenzie Youth Education Fund with a gift of £10,000, and the J R McKenzie Trust, two years later with a further gift of £100,000. South Island retailer Sir James Hay set up the J L Hay Charitable Trust in 1959 while fisheries baron Sir Clifford Skeggs established the Skeggs Foundation to promote sporting endeavour, retailer David Levene supported hospices, was a patron of Outward Bound and created a charitable trust to assist other worthy organisations. In 1960 Sir John Ilott, who helped create the advertising industry, not only donated his entire and extensive art collection to the National Art Gallery, now part of Te Papa, but established The John Ilott Charitable Trust to specifically improve, among other things, literacy, parenting, sexual education and women re-entering the workforce. Meanwhile, engineer Brian Perry set up the Perry Foundation in 1976 to support a host of community initiatives, and in 1977 construction tycoon Sir Neil Isaac created the Isaac Wildlife Trust to promote conservation.

Other laureates turned their attention to higher learning. Dairy industrialist and investor Sir Douglas Goodfellow was a long time supporter and generous donor to the St Kentigern college in Auckland, established and funded a postgraduate chair in general practice at the Auckland Medical School, and the Douglas Goodfellow Scholarship in Engineering. Showing a similar desire to promote innovation at university level, biotech pioneer Trevor Scott donated $1 million to establish the T D Scott Professorial Chair in Urology at Otago University which then lead to the formation of a trust raising millions more for medical research and teaching. Tony Falkenstein showed his commitment to building the capacity of the next generation by underwriting $300,000 in 2003 to establish the country's first business secondary school at Onehunga High School. He followed that up by giving the school an additional $1 million donation of Just Water shares. He also gave similar donations to the University of Auckland business school and the Unitec school of business management.

Former Onehunga High School principal Deidre Shea said: "Tony has been, and is, an inspiration. He has his sights firmly fixed on our young people fulfilling their potential in terms of entrepreneurial, creative thinking and contributing positively to our economy and our world. Tony has created a unique opportunity for young people to learn about Business and entrepreneurship, while at secondary school. He is a New Zealander who has put his money where his mouth is, and he is making a difference."

Sir Stephen Tindall established the Tindall Foundation to improve family and community life and foster enterprise, while Sir John Todd chairs the Todd Foundation which also focuses its efforts on funding for children and their families. In 1990 Sir John helped establish Philanthropy New Zealand, an umbrella group bringing together private philanthropists, trusts, foundations, businesses and others to encourage even more focused grants to support New Zealand communities. Its vision: "We believe the way in which we carry out our philanthropy - whether we give money, time, or experience - can build social capital in our communities and will enrich Aotearoa New Zealand."

In addition to the laureates who created trusts and foundations, are all those who simply gave donations personally to a host of causes. For instance, food magnate Sir Jack Butland was seen as the leading public benefactor of his day in the mid 20th century, donating an estimated $500,000 personally to a variety of causes. The reach of these laureates extends across the country and into every level of the community - children, families and those in need, education, arts, medicine, the environment and all manner of small community initiatives. If you could tally up the quantum of money these laureates have contributed to society, it would be in the hundreds of millions of dollars.

In reviewing the actions of these business greats, it is interesting to consider a rule of measure Dame Wendy Pye suggests be applied to business leaders: "You are judged on your credibility and your accountability to the people in the community."

She goes on to define great business leaders by saying: "By true leadership I mean people who have truly succeeded in the world, not necessarily by making lots of money, but by contributing something back to society and by making a difference to the world."

Laureate and meat processing entrepreneur Graeme Lowe was another generous philanthropist during his lifetime, passing those values to his son, Andy Lowe, who, when talking about the legacy of his father, similarly highlighted that community obligation. "Graeme's always instilled in me that he's only got where he is in life through the support of the local community. He's always taught me that giving back is very important."

Pharmaceutical industrialist Sir Graeme Douglas agrees. Looking back on one of the moments from his business life which has brought him greatest pleasure, he said it was not the making of the money, but the spending of it.. He and his wife gave $3m towards an MRI scanner at Starship Children's Hospital, which remains the hospital's largest single personal donation. They have donated a lot more, but choose to do so with minimum fuss. "It gives you that wonderful warm feeling when some of those good people with their very unwell children have the facility of the MRI to assist in the diagnosis and treatment of their children," he said.

Make no mistake, Sir Graeme is an uncompromising, hard-nosed businessman through and through. All businessmen have an obligation to concentrate on profit first, he said. But then, crucially he says they have an equal obligation to consider how they can benefit the wider society.

"If they are successful and they come up with appropriate dividends then I also think it becomes part of their civic responsibility to review favourably requests for philanthropy."

Civic responsibility is an interesting phrase. How does he define it? "It covers a great spectrum of activity, it is really a whole society, if we don't all have some sense of civic responsibility then its not far away from the next step of anarchy – without wishing to sound too dramatic. If you have a business that is indeed profitable and you have the appropriate funds available then they should go to help where the state, whether local or national, is unable for one reason or another to assist. We are enthusiasts on things like Starship and hospices, the Cancer Society and Heart Foundation where government help is usually in the form of a subsidy or sometimes none at all."

He then goes on to express his ability to offer support as a form of good fortune to himself. "If you are in a position to do something concrete about what's happening then I think those who can participate in some form of philanthropy are quite fortunate." It is remarkably similar to a sentiment expressed by Dame Wendy Pye who said: "I feel that if you have the opportunity in life to go out and do something positive - and yes, you have also got to make profits and employ people - but if you have the opportunity to do good, what a great opportunity."

Sir Peter Leitch – best known as the Mad Butcher – is another renowned for his generousity. And like many of the laureates, he is reluctant to talk about it. Few of these business leaders involve themselves in what they do for the public acclaim. Many end up supporting causes or giving away millions quietly, without fanfare. It is a curious situation for Sir Peter, a man with marketing in his blood. With the business brand so intimately tied to his own persona, he could be accused of being a shameless self promoter – his constant barracking for his beloved rugby league boosts his business profile as much as it benefits the sport. Yet what is not truly appreciated is that his hand goes into his own pocket to support a bewildering array of charity, mostly done quietly. "I don't do things for recognition. That's not my go mate. I just do it because its me," he said. Part of this is because he is unusually accessible. His email address is readily available. Email him and you are as likely to find yourself on the end of the line within moments, night or day - a daunting prospect for some to suddenly find themselves talking to a figure they near idolise. But he is spontaneous and prefers to talk – and make the human connection. "Even today with my profile you can ring me," he said.

"I don't see myself as a philanthropist. I see myself as a person who has helped out where I can because I just do what I can. You look at the people like the super rich, they give shit loads away. I am not in that league." Looking back on what he has done, he cites his help for those devastated by the Christchurch earthquake as a highpoint. The other was work with a charitable trust he founded, which in one project worked alongside Counties Manukau District Health Board to open a hospital surgery theatre on the weekend (unheard of at the time), bring in doctors, and put on transport to bring every family with a child suffering glue ear to the clinic to have instant operations to insert grommets. These small tubes drain the ear and allow the children to hear, relieved of pain and able to concentrate on listening and learning. Over two weekends, Leitch and his volunteers blitzed the entire glue ear waiting list of south Auckland. The benefits to the health board in such a poor area of eliminating such an extensive waiting list were enormous. The benefits for those children were incalculable.

So why does he respond so readily to so many who approach him? "I just think it's a personal thing, you just want to help out where you can. We've done our bit."

This illustrates that philanthropy in business is much more than desiccated Miltonian arguments of capitalism versus social conscience. It's a far more personal and primal issue, about authenticity and private values. It is something that is engrained within the laureates, as the people they are. If you reflect back to Dame Wendy Pye's comments on business ethics, they are in marked contrast with those who are avaricious and in business with the sole aim of enriching themselves and enjoying a luxury lifestyle.

Anne Norman is another who, like Sir Peter Leitch, will often be moved by impulse. She and husband David, give regularly to charities associated with leukaemia and blood cancer . These choices arose out of personal experience, both had siblings who died of cancer as children. "We did feel it was important to give to one charity, it made a lot of sense to us to focus on one charity. It was one we could both relate to. But we are always being asked to give money and it is hard to say no." They respond when they can. "The other day I read about somebody who was doing a lot with music and so we gave some money to them. It was only a small amount but to them it was a lot of money."

And like Sir Peter, Norman finds it hard to express fully what motivates her to engage in philanthropy. We should remember, any of these Business Hall of Fame laureates could simply keep their hard-earned money, take overseas holidays, buy luxury cars. But they don't. "Sometimes things just happen and you think 'golly, I would like to help them.' There is no compulsion. It is simply nice to be able to do it. You just want to do it because you can - because you can." And in this, Norman says, they are no different to the ordinary kiwi — it is just a matter of scale. "I think New Zealanders are really generous." She points to the response to the appeals to assist Samoa after the 2009 tsunami. In the Norman's Farmers stores they raised enough in donations to build a new library.

Norman also brings a different dimension to the issue, one of 'internal philanthropy,' which recognises the social good inherent in ethically-operated businesses. "We do have our charity, but I also do think that we employ 10,000 people. We are investing in 10,000 people and by having a strong company we are investing in their families. They rely on us, we give them a safe environment to work in and if they are doing a good job, their jobs are secure." She is right. Each person on her payroll is a person servicing a mortgage, putting food on the table, and rippling that economic benefit out to the wider community. It is a philosophical approach to business which is heartening to hear, treating a business with a sense of stewardship, running a business as a sustainable entity embedded in a community – not as a profit-oriented company divorced from society, a cash cow for personal enlargement. It is through this ethical approach to business that important social innovations can take place, no less significant than the charitable philanthropy. An example is Sir John Illot, who we referenced above for his charitable bequests, who was also the first to establish a comprehensive superannuation plan, arrange for long Christmas holidays and initiate optional flexible hours of work for his staff. Anne Norman is at the forefront of another modern issue of the workplace, that of work life balance. Ninety percent of her retail outlet employees are women, most often with families, necessitating the often difficult task of juggling between two sides of life. Norman: "We understand they have two lives, they have their business life and they have their family life and we try to make sure we accommodate both." It is an approach to business which must be lauded as equally as any overtly charitable work.

Through the staggering generosity of the bequests throughout their lives, and even in death, Thomas Macarthy, Marianne Caughey, Sir Peter Leitch, Sir Graeme Douglas and all those other great laureates embody the Bhagwati virtues: Creating personal wealth through a business that was uncompromising in striving for profitable growth based on customer value, no matter how that ruffled established rivals, but also ensuring that this prosperity was spread wide for the greater benefit of the community.

If we can be allowed the licence to coin a new phrase, it is what can be called *cognisant capitalism*, meaning that wealth creation is best allied with a moral compass and a shrewd appreciation that no business is an island. Smart businesses actively engage in a virtuous cycle of contributing to the greater good of society, understanding that a society growing stronger provides much more fertile opportunity for that business to also endure and flourish.

To return to TG Macarthy and the High Tea held in 2012 to celebrate, not his death, but the founding of that great charity he bequeathed to the nation: Governor General Mataparae made an apt quote with the words of the 19th century British Prime Minister, Benjamin Disraeli: "The legacy of heroes is the memory of a great name and the inheritance of a great example." Many have followed Macarthy's example. May they continue to do so.

MARIANNE CAUGHEY SMITH PRESTON: Practical Philanthropy in Action

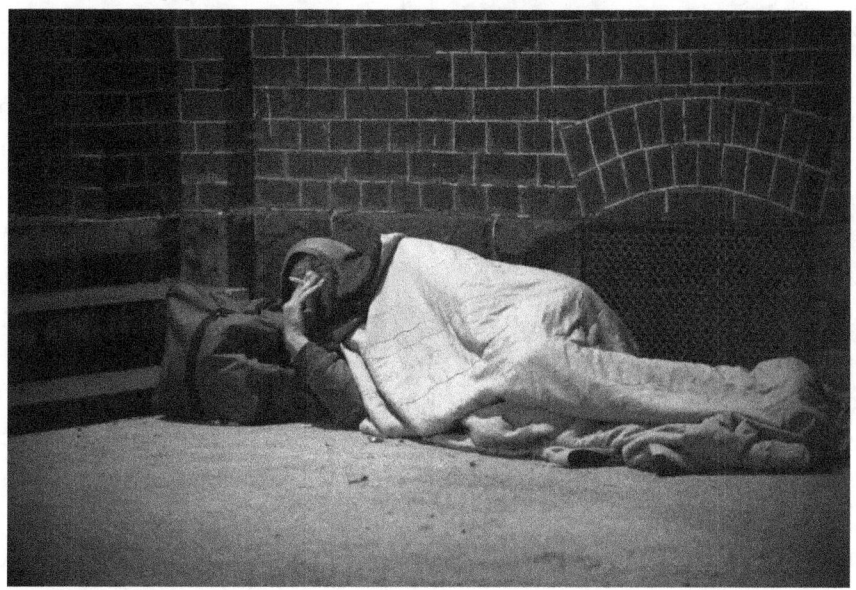

Marianne Caughey Smith Preston (1851–1938), co-founder of Auckland high fashion store Smith and Caughey is described by journalist, historian and women's advocate Sandra Coney as: "An enigmatic and very private person."

But from what is known of her, significant lessons can be learnt – the power of networking to see you through tough times, a long-term, intergenerational view on wealth creation and retention, but above all the role of social philanthropy as a corollary to business.

Unusually for her time, she was a self made businesswoman, who grew to immense wealth from economic ground zero, on the back of hard work. Yet she rates amongst the most generous of New Zealand benefactors, representing the best of traditional philanthropy.

Marianne Caughey was born at Portaferry near Belfast, Ireland, the youngest daughter of the seven children of grocer James Caughey.

She married William Smith, who worked with her brother Andrew at a

Belfast drapery store. They soon left Ireland though and set up a drapery firm in New York, then returned to Belfast for less than a year, before sailing to New Zealand.

They arrived in Auckland in early 1880, and she opened her own store on the corner of Queen Street and what is now Airedale Street in Auckland, called Smith's Cheap Drapery Warehouse. Because the new firm could not support husband and wife, Smith initially worked for another draper, but it flourished and by 1881 Caughey's store was doing so well he was able to join her.

The shop's success was built on a policy of high turnover through low retail margins, embodied in the mottos, 'Small profits and quick returns' and 'A nimble sixpence rather than a slow shilling'.

Of note, the store fostered a Maori clientele by advertising in the Maori-language newspaper Te Korimako .

At the same time her brother Andrew Caughey, had emigrated to New Zealand. The story goes that the business he was by then working at suffered a serious fire. There were allegations of insurance fraud and appalled by the dishonesty, he resigned and turned his back on the old world.

He also abandoned his trade, becoming instead a Methodist minister. He was given a ministry to the south of Auckland and travelled from village to village, riding a horse cross country carrying the word of God to pioneers. For three years he drove himself hard, then suffered a breakdown in health.

Caughey and William Smith took him in while he convalesced and persuaded him to once more join Smith in a partnership in their business. The name of Smith and Caughey was born in Auckland. In

1884 Smith and Caughey moved to its prime site on the western side of Queen Street.

From the beginning they were successful and the entire Caughey clan moved out to join them, father James, a brother and two sisters. Marianne Caughey was not a partner in the new firm of Smith & Caughey, which is more reflective of the social mores of the time than her ability or role.

But the growth of the business over the next 30 years owed much to the efforts of all three family members. They pushed the boundaries of established business policies to grow their firm. For instance they began direct purchasing from overseas markets, to the anger of local wholesalers. In 1902 Marianne and William went on a buying trip to India and in 1908 and 1913 she made solo buying trips to Britain. By 1900 William and Andrew had formed a limited liability company. Marianne was one of eight shareholders when Smith died in 1912 leaving her a widow with a young adopted child.

But she maintained an active role in the business, appointed a director in 1916, a position she held until her death.

Today, more than 130 years later, Smith & Caughey's is one of New Zealand's top department stores and still largely family owned. That underlines a key trait of the successfully wealthy dynastic businesses, which the Caughey's can thank their early matriarch for. Marianne Caughey left 47% of the shares in a charitable trust, so it could not be broken up, thus giving the family a sense of intergenerational financial cohesion around an asset to steward over the long term. In contrast consider some of the prominent family business names of just a few decades ago who took their companies public or acquired debt to expand.

Like her late husband and brother, Marianne Caughey was a staunch Christian and was part of a network, particularly of Methodist traders in Auckland, who helped each other.

This Christian ethos also saw her give generously to welfare and educational causes. She and her husband started the Helping Hand Mission, from which evolved the Auckland Central Mission.

In 1907 Caughey and her husband gave Auckland Hospital Board a 1.4ha property at Ellerslie containing a two-storey house as a convalescent home for women and children. She and her brother also gifted the Methodist Church a property in Mt Albert, Auckland, for an orphanage. After Smith died, she even gave their Herne Bay home to the Salvation Army for an orphanage.

She funded the building of a hospital and chapel at Wesley College, Paerata. She was also a leading supporter of the Methodist Mission in the Solomon Islands and the YMCA and YWCA in Auckland and created other parks in the city.

In 1932, she remarried, to Raymond Preston, a minister, and acquired her multi-barreled surname Marianne Caughey Smith Preston. Her generous public spirit was recognised in 1935 when she was honoured with an MBE.

The philanthropy continued after death. Under her will she bequeathed her shareholding in Smith & Caughey Ltd to The Marianne Caughey Smith-Preston Memorial Rest Homes Trust Board and created what is one of her most enduring legacies. Established in 1950, the board provides quality rest home, dementia and hospital care for about 220 clients in Remuera, Auckland.

+ *Sources for this profile include: business journalist and historian Graeme Hunt and the Dictionary of New Zealand Biography, entry written by Sandra Coney.*

DOUGLAS GOODFELLOW: A Legacy

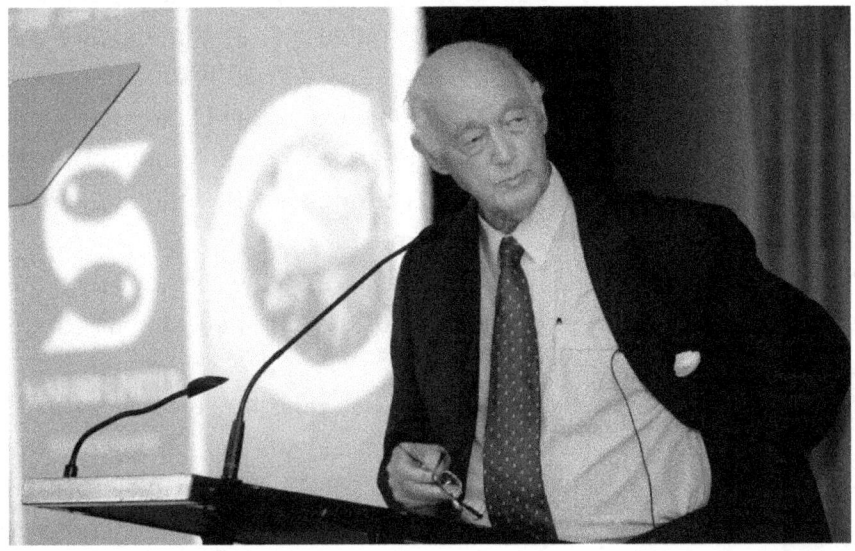

Once New Zealand's richest man, Douglas Goodfellow dedicated much of his family's wealth to educating the next generation of physicians, engineers and business people.

A hallmark of this business great has always been his tireless energy. Goodfellow, OBE, even in his 90s, still managed his business interests from the Auckland home he shared with his wife of 59 years, Judith.

He preferred to work into the night, rising late in the morning when he received a file of business papers then regularly conferred via telephone with his son, Bruce Goodfellow, who had taken up his father's Amalgamated Dairies offices in Auckland.

But even if he was not constantly occupied by his business and philanthropic dealings, it is a good bet Douglas Goodfellow would not feel inclined to speak about his remarkable success. He topped the Rich List in 1994 but a year later, his wealth had been transferred to family trusts. He was one laureate who even shunned the recognition that came with his Business Hall of Fame induction, directing comment instead to his son, Bruce.

The Amalgamated Dairies office is also modest - it has not been redecorated since about 1975 when the company moved in. Bruce Goodfellow describes himself as a workaholic like his father, and says they prefer to concentrate on business rather than interior design.

The office he has inherited from his father is filled with memories of Amalgamated's exporting heyday. A large mahogany desk is covered in papers, with a silver tea service at the ready. Bruce's addition to the office - a circular wooden table - is surrounded by four soft, brown armchairs, more suited to a living room.

"I remember when I joined the company in 1980 the company secretary said to me that every ship going out of those ports had some of our product on it, " Bruce says.

In one corner stands a flag proudly displaying the company slogan - "Amal. The Mark of Quality". Next to it, and with pride of place on the wall, is a framed newspaper clipping of Douglas' father, William Goodfellow, kneeling to receive his knighthood from the Queen during the 1953 royal tour.

It was Sir William who took the family into the dairy industry, founding the Waikato Dairy Company in 1909, after a customer of his general merchant business defaulted on an order of dairy equipment. In 1910, he added "Co-operative" to the company name and set about building a model that would sustain dairy expansion for the next century.

Sir William's belief in production economies of scale and his zest for a co-ordinated overseas marketing plan that was ahead of its time were the forerunners for his son's divergence into meat, live breeding stock, seafood and, more recently, investment shareholdings.

Douglas Goodfellow was born in 1917, in Hamilton, and went to Fairfield School before shifting to Mt Roskill Primary and Auckland Grammar School. He spent a year at Auckland Medical School and then joined the Royal Navy and saw World War II action in the Mediterranean Sea.

After the war he worked for Empire Dairies' London office, a partnership between Sir William's Amalgamated Dairies and the Australian Producers' Wholesale Co- operative Federation to drive sales in the

Mother Country. He met his Australian-born wife and they returned to New Zealand in 1951 to marry.

Sir William's efforts to get New Zealand dairy producers working together had run their course and Empire Dairies was eventually sold to the New Zealand Dairy Products Marketing Commission. But Douglas continued to seek trading opportunities around the world. He brought Lada cars and potash to New Zealand from the Soviet Union during the 1960s. Amalgamated also exported fruit, vegetables and meats, and Douglas continued to govern his father's interests in dairy, refrigeration and clothing.

He has been a director of New Zealand Insurance, New Zealand Farmers Fertiliser Company (now Nufarm), and was chairman of seafood company Sanford for more than 30 years. Douglas and Amalgamated Dairies own almost 40 per cent of Sanford and helped build the company into the country's second largest fishing operation.

Amalgamated also owned half of the country's third largest fishing company, Amaltal, a joint venture with the Talley family of Motueka, but sold out to the Talleys in 2005 for an undisclosed sum.

But business is only half of what Douglas Goodfellow devotes himself to. He's best known for supporting educational institutions such as Saint Kentigern School and College in Auckland. Sir William was among nine original founders of the Saint Kentigern Trust Board in 1949. They sought to realise the Presbyterian Church principle that knowledge should be used "for the Glory of God and the benefit of mankind" and involve "a proper discipline of mind and body and a life of service to others".

Ten years later when Douglas sent his sons, Bruce and Peter, to the preparatory school which had just opened in Remuera, he also joined the school's board. He sat on the trust board since 1962 and was chairman from 1965 to 2000. The fingerprint of his "life of service to others" can be seen across the grounds of both the school and college.

Bruce Goodfellow took over from his father as chairman of the trust board in 2000. Douglas' other son, Peter, also has directorships in the family's holdings and served as National Party president.

Douglas' contributions to education extend into the tertiary sector. To mark the 50th anniversary of Amalgamated Dairies, and also in memory of his father, Douglas funded the Goodfellow unit in the School of Population Health at Auckland University. He also established a postgraduate chair in general practice at Auckland Medical School and the Richard Maclaurin Goodfellow chair in theology.

He was instrumental in setting up trusts and heading governance for the purposes of medical research and care of the elderly.

"It all comes from the basis of his faith being the Presbyterian Church, which is very much hard work, study and academics, and giving back to society," Bruce says. "When he's involved with charities he gets involved with them personally and gives of his time. Business was different in those days; it was much more to scale, it wasn't as tight to manage as what businesses are today."

Douglas' hardworking attitude extended to the roughly biennial holidays that the family spent in Judith's hometown of Melbourne, Bruce says.

"We'd go for four or five weeks, but I can remember in Melbourne he'd go to work every single day - he'd catch the train in because there was an office in Melbourne."

Bruce says his father's reputation for commitment and honest business dealings began to precede him. "We had a very good profile and reputation out in the market as people to deal with. You needed honesty and integrity in business.

"Because of some of the shareholdings that he had he was approached to sell out at higher prices, but he would say, 'No, everybody's got to be treated fairly and all shareholders must receive the same price'."

+ Sources for this profile were a one to one interview by William Mace with Bruce Goodfellow, son of Douglas Goodfellow, and a short note from the man himself.

Chapter Six

THE FUTURE OF BUSINESS

As a 17 year old student at Tauranga Girls College Izzi Morris was adamant she would never consider business as a career.

"My impression was that it was too stressful, too boring, too cut-throat and, frankly, there were just too many men in black suits, " she said. It is probably an attitude not too uncommon among teenagers slogging through the final years of school.

But Izzi's outlook on life changed.

And in 2011 she found herself standing on a stage addressing the gathered alumni, supporters and newly minted laureates of the Fairfax Media NZ Business Hall of Fame gala awards dinner. "That girl who refused to ever be involved in commerce a year ago is now standing here talking to the most influential businesspeople in the country, going on to study commerce at university and has a huge passion and drive for a career in business, " she said in her speech to the laureates.

What brought about this change?

"The power of an experience."

Izzi was persuaded by a passionate teacher to take part in the Lion Foundation Young Enterprise Scheme run by the charitable Young Enterprise Trust, whose vision is to grow a more prosperous New Zealand by helping educate school students about business. It sets about work in a practical manner, having students establish and operate mini businesses. Under the YES programme students have to design a product, negotiate with suppliers, sell stock, and complete budgets and cashflows. They become immersed, not in the theory, but in the reality of business decisions. The process nurtures an all important quality – enterprise. Being enterprising is essential regardless of whether a young person will go on to set up their own company or work for someone else, whether the organisation they ultimately work for or lead is large or small, or whether it is a commercial business, government agency or not for profit organisation.. It is about identifying, valuing and capturing

Izzi Morris [right] and her YES team

opportunities. It is about taking ownership, exercising initiative and showing leadership. It is the only way an individual, a business and a country can move forward.

For Izzi, the pivotal point was her experience founding with her friends Tiger Enterprise, which produced Tiger Multi Bags, reusable, machine-washable lunch and toiletry bags that come in about 20 different designs. It opened her eyes to the thrills, demands, and potentials of business.

"The YES experience has been (as cheesy as it sounds) life changing. Prior to this year I would have never considered studying or working in the commerce field, but my experience competing in the Young Enterprise Scheme has changed that. The hands on nature of starting your own business, learning through trial and error what does and doesn't work, the highs of negotiating a deal with a retailers and the frustrations of dealing with unreliable manufacturers - it gives you a real taste of what it's like," she said.

She discovered she was actually good at business. Her YES business team became the regional winner for the Bay of Plenty. She herself got the highest mark of all YES students who sat the Young Enterprise Exam administered by AUT University and she was named the AUT Young Enterprise Scholar of the Year for 2012. All of which saw her selected from 2900 YES students throughout the country to deliver the keynote speech of the 2011 Business Hall of Fame laureate induction – which then compounded the impact on her of exposure to business. Standing on that podium before the good and the great of New Zealand's business community delivering a sharp and incisive speech highlighted her abilities to those in the auditorium and she was approached by one of the senior managers at KPMG, who offered her a position working there over the summer in the Business Strategy department. Another experience to relish.

Izzi, at the time of writing this, had so reversed her initial diffidence regarding business studies that she planned to study Commerce at Auckland University in a conjoint Science degree with a likely major in International Business/Economics and Statistics.

The YES experience, that first Tiger taste of business, has had therefore an ongoing, profound impact on her outlook, ability to network and future prospects. "My involvement with YES has given me some amazing opportunities. I had the chance to compete in Hong Kong in August at the JA/FedEx Asia-Pacific International Trade Challenge with five other students from New Zealand. The experience of seeing the way students from other countries tackle the same business issues was a great. I learnt so much and I now consider the rest of the Kiwi team some of my closest friends. Even post-Hong Kong we will often run business ideas past each other over Skype or Facebook. I have a lot to thank the YE Trust for."

Izzi has become a passionate advocate for the power of experience. Her speech to the laureates was a rallying call for business people to take a greater stake in providing experience for those seeking to carve out a start in business. It made those listening sit up and take notice. There is a history of strong speeches from the youth ambassadors of the Young Enterprise scheme. In 2008 seventeen-year-old Alex Mackenzie similarly stunned those assembled with a speech attacking modern business ethics. The message from the Westlake Boys High School student was very reminiscent of the point made by Dame Wendy Pye earlier in this work, chiding business leaders that their actions set an example that the next generation observed and learnt from. He reminded them of the world we live in. "A world where you can get a pizza delivered faster to your house than an ambulance. A world where efficiency and profit are elevated above ethics and morals. And often, it is both the political and business leaders of the world that are encouraging this new morality; that doing the right thing no longer matters, that the ends justify the means. It is consequences, not morals, that dictate courses of action. How absurd! What topsy-turvy world are we living in? For when leadership is corrupt, society inevitably becomes corrupt. Think about it. Tell a young child every day that right is right and wrong is wrong, and eventually they will understand. But likewise, tell a young child every day that wrong is right and right is wrong, and now you have a problem on your hands."

But, said Alex, the laureates of the business hall of fame were proof that there is hope. "For I believe that the greatest aspect of these laureates is not that they are incredible business people, but very simply, that they are incredible. How they can achieve such a wealth of unrivalled business achievements and yet stick to such a strong set of values in such a morally decaying world is what really fills me to the brim with patriotism. My New Zealand leaders are competing at the same level as anyone else in the world, yet they are acting with a social and a moral compass. What motivational role models! Few among us here could say that we have always done what was right, always taken the morally superior path. Oftentimes when we meet a fork in the pathway of morals we steer not towards what is right, but what is easy. These laureates have showed us that, as human beings, we can make a conscious decision to be better people. And I think this is the pinnacle of nobility. They have somehow found time in their inordinately busy schedule to take interest in the wider community and help others without personal gain. And I think that this is one of the most admirable things we can do as a people."

And just like Izzi, Alex paid tribute to the strength of the Young Enterprise scheme: "Nothing else is available to someone of my age that will so ably and realistically imitate the running of a business, and that is because - you are running a business!"

The experience of these teenagers is proof of why initiatives such as the Young Enterprise scheme need support, and why much of the forward thinking philanthropic endeavour of the business leader laureates has been towards support and development of youth and education. Tony Falkenstein, who has very visibly backed efforts to improve the teaching of business skills and financial literacy, is a great advocate of the benefits of encouraging all young people to experience business.

New Zealand teenagers can be world beaters when it comes to business brains and innovation, he says. Even those from the poorest families and lowest decile schools can foot it internationally if given the opportunity. Of all his business achievements he cites his most satisfying as going to New York with 15 students from the Onehunga Business School, some who had never been overseas before. They attended a lecture at a US university and during class break out groups transformed from awed nervousness to dominating discussion. "They thought everything in the USA has to be bigger and brighter, but they realised they were better than the US kids." He says our country has a huge potential resource in entrepreneurial skill amongst our young people, but we are not mining it effectively because we do not take enough effort to teach financial literacy and business skills. At the moment there are young people who have the raw potential to go on and be business entrepreneurs, but they never even consider it because they haven't been brought up in a household where people talk business.

"It would just never come to their minds that they could be in business." He says New Zealand is therefore hobbled – we only have business people coming from a small sector of society. "It's like picking the All Black team only from Invercargill. If you said 0.1% of New Zealanders have an enormous talent for entrepreneurship, then we're missing out on a lot of them." And it is something we should focus on in a co-ordinated way, just as the Young Enterprise scheme does. "I think its like developing a product. This is a niche that I think New Zealand could say 'hey we want to lead this'. "My passion is if we can teach business skills early, that's the path to economic prosperity. In New Zealand young people just don't have financial skills. Financial literacy has been dumbed down and teachers see business as a necessary evil."

Izzi shows us the hope of the future. Her story is what good business is about – putting back into the young of today, inspiring them, setting challenges and goals and helping to create the next generation of business leaders which will move this country and our economy onwards. It is succession planning on a social scale.

That Speech:

Here then is the full script of the 2011 speech by Izzi Morris which provides tips for both existing businesses and those wanting to break into the business world about how the two worlds can help each other on a practical level:

Good evening Your Excellencies, distinguished guests, sponsors, ladies and gentlemen.

I believe that numbers tell stories. In this room we have 150 of the most influential and successful businesspeople in the country. One thing you have in common, is that you have all been leaders in NZ business. Another thing you have in common is that you are all Baby Boomers - a generation that youth today look up to – but also a generation we are scared of.

No - it's not your fashion choices, your 80's hair styles or your lack of friends on Facebook that scare us. It is the future cost of your mobility scooters, rest homes and medical bills which instill fear.

Yes - in the next 10, 20, 30 years - me, and my generation, are going to be the people supporting you. And this is where numbers tell a very interesting story.

• When the majority of you were born, there were around 7 people supporting every one person over the age of 65.

• Today that figure has dropped a little – 5 of you are working to support one retiree.

• By the time all of you have officially retired – which I'm guessing will be in 20 years or so – only three people will be working to support every one of you.

• I am going to be one of those people.

This tells a story of a very different New Zealand to the one you have experienced. The aging population is not a new phenomenon. It's been in the media a lot lately with discussion around whether the superannuation age should be raised or means tested.

In my opinion, as a young person, the more important discussion we should be having is how can we make those three people who will be supporting you as efficient, productive and effective as possible?

In the context of tonight — how can we create great young businesspeople? Studying in a classroom can teach you theory — but there is no better way of creating passionate, driven and creative businesspeople than letting them experience it for themselves.

This time a year ago I said I would never consider business as a career. My impression was that it was too stressful, too boring, too cut throat, and frankly there were just too many men in black suits.

It was only because of a very passionate teacher that I became involved in the Young Enterprise Scheme. In this competition we have to create a real business. Negotiate with real suppliers, create real websites, sell real stock, complete real budgets and cashflows. I very nearly had a real heart attack when we found out we hadn't included GST in our manufacturing cost!

What we have been doing is making real mistakes and learning real lessons from them.

That girl who refused to ever be involved in commerce a year ago is now standing here talking to the most influential businesspeople in the country, going on study commerce at university and has a huge passion and drive for a career in business.

That is the power of an experience.

In this room there are 150 business people with lifetimes of experience. Experience that should be shared with young people.

One thing running a business has taught me is to be clear about what you want — so tonight I am going to be very clear, and ask you to invest. To invest in young people in New Zealand. It can be your money - but to be honest we would benefit more from an investment of your time and your expertise. Teach us what you know. Let us experience your businesses. Let us share in that same passion you have for your companies. Let's accelerate the learning process.

Today I want to leave you with three ways you can invest in young people:

1. Mentoring – I know – not exactly an original idea and no doubt you all mentor people within your businesses. But there is a very real opportunity to extend that further. In programmes like Young Enterprise – every team has a mentor who works with them, for say one hour a week, on their business. Realistically, I know as leaders of businesses you may not have the time to do this – but your employees could, if you just encourage them and give them the time to be involved.

2. Link up with your local college, university or polytechnic. Your involvement can be as small or as big as you want to make it. On a larger scale – how great would it be if we had business schools within every college in the country like Tony Falkenstein has done with Onehunga High School. Rangitoto College has created a smaller scale business school to link students up with local business. For example, HSBC invite students along when they have presentations from visiting economists or experts. Some businesses are linking up with schools as part of their Social Responsibility programmes and assign staff to work with the business classes. Westpac invited students to work on their stall at the Mystery Creek Fieldays. One local business is regularly inviting students to their product launches. At the practical end of the workforce, MIT have set up Trade Academies in the past few years where students split their time between school, studying their trade at MIT and getting practical work experience 1 day a week.

3. Offer job opportunities in holidays – I have just found the university calendar for next year, and I'm astonished that the amount of time we spend on holiday is almost equal to the amount of time spent studying! These holidays are an ideal time to accelerate that learning. Whether it is employing a student for two weeks to work on a project or an annual internship every summer – by giving young people a small experience of a real working business, you give them a huge insight into the world of business.

I am sure you've all planned well for your retirement – and don't really need the help of those three people. But there are many Baby Boomers for whom that is not the case. You are in a unique position to make a difference.

You sit here today because you are some of the most passionate, driven and successful business people in New Zealand over the past 30 years. My question is – what investment will you make to help create the passionate, driven businesspeople in the next 30 years.

SIR GRAEME DOUGLAS: Boundless energy

It started with a cough, $500 in capital and a desire for a big challenge. That was the genesis back in 1957 for what became Douglas Pharmaceuticals with an annual turnover of about $145 million.

Most people would agree founder Sir Graeme Douglas rose to the challenge.

The chemist started with one small pharmacy in west Auckland's Te Atatu at a time when New Zealand laws prohibited ownership of more than one shop. Chemists, or pharmacists as they're more widely known today, made up their own medications.

For Sir Graeme, manufacturing naturally followed. He started selling his own brand of products, beginning with a cough syrup called Kofsin. The next step was to begin importing niche pharmaceuticals and packaging them at his shop before distributing them to other pharmacists. And so was born Douglas Pharmaceuticals. The shop was turning over $2 million when Sir Graeme sold it in the late 1970s to focus on the new business, which shifted to new offices and warehousing in Henderson, also in west Auckland.

Kofsin had a good run, says Sir Graeme from the group's now considerably expanded Henderson headquarters. "We considered the active ingredient, which is noscapine, could be offered to advantage to the New Zealand public."

Problem was the stuff wasn't at all pleasant to taste, an issue that vexed him greatly at the time. "It's a very difficult active ingredient to make palatable and if you don't make cough mixtures palatable, then you immediately have problems with children."

Their hard work on making the cough elixir taste better paid off when it was well received by consumers. However, he made it for only five years before marketplace consolidation put a stop to it. There were only two manufacturers of noscapine, both in Europe. "One of them sold the company and left a monopoly supplier who, like many monopolies, pushed up the prices. It was unviable, " he says.

Initial growth of the pharmaceutical manufacturer was slow but by the early 1980s Douglas Pharmaceuticals had about 40 products and a $5m turnover. By the late 80s revenue leapt to $25m - 90 per cent earned domestically. Ten years later it was clocking up sales of more than $70m a year. By 2011 , $85m of its $145m annual turnover was derived from exporting to more than 35 countries and it produced more than 455 million tablets, 270,000 litres and 31 metric tonnes of pharmaceutical medicines, liquids and creams.

After decades of expansion, it might be fair to ask whether Sir Graeme has much left in business to get excited about. But the group is still trying to break new ground. After 10 years of trying to break into the United States market, in January 2011 the company had its prescription acne medication isotretinoin approved by the Food and Drugs Administration. It was believed to be the first Kiwi- developed human medicine to be approved for use in the US. It was a big deal - the US accounts for more than half of the world's total pharmaceutical spend, which is estimated by market research company IMS Health to reach almost US$1.1 trillion by 2015.

The newly-approved product is sold in New Zealand as Oratane and is the group's biggest export product. It is also market leader in Spain, Austria, Germany and Mexico. Used to treat severe acne, it is sold as Myorisan in the US.

"We have several [products] following that are happily making much faster progress. It couldn't be any bloody slower," said Sir Graeme in typically pithy fashion. Getting FDA approval is just the first step though, rather than a licence to print money. "We've now got to market it and convince the consumers, starting with the prescribing dermatologists, to the pharmacists who purchase the product to dispense that, indeed, this is a product of integrity.

"The supply chain is certainly very, very important, particularly in markets like the US."

Throw in the considerable marketing budget and the company has racked up millions on the application before selling a single unit.

At 83, at the time of this interview, he was still content to stay at the helm as managing director. But one of Sir Graeme and wife Ngaire's two sons has worked his way through the firm. Jeff, 53, who holds a commerce degree, joined the business aged 20 and has been with the company since. He's now the managing director of the group's export division.

"He's obviously got more energy than I have so he drives it harder. He's a great salesman, " Sir Graeme says. "I lean toward the manufacturing facility."

His second son, Richard, 50, is a head and neck surgeon [formerly called an ear, nose, throat surgeon] with a private practice in Auckland.

Sir Graeme was knighted in 2010 for services to philanthropy and athletics and in 1988 was appointed a member of the New Zealand Order of Merit for services to the New Zealand pharmaceutical industry. Both he and his wife have given back significantly to the community, one of the criteria for becoming a Hall of Fame laureate. They've provided funding for a research fellow for the Neurological Foundation and bought lifesaving equipment and an MRI scanner for Starship children's hospital which, at $3m, remains the hospital's largest single, personal donation. Sir Graeme also supports the West Auckland

Hospice, Medical Air Abroad, the Heart Foundation, Cancer Society, the Liggins Institute (University of Auckland's cancer research institute) and the Oliver Smales Memorial Trust which educates and trains therapists and nursing staff working with children and youth in Hawke's Bay. Sir Graeme was an Auckland representative shot-putter and also supports the Waitakere City Athletics Club.

He has been one of the major sponsors of the Waitakere City Stadium, sited just opposite his company precincts, and the field and all-weather running track bear his name.

+ Sources for this profile were a one to one interview by Nick Krause with Sir Graeme Douglas.

SIR JOHN ILOTT: A Restless Energy

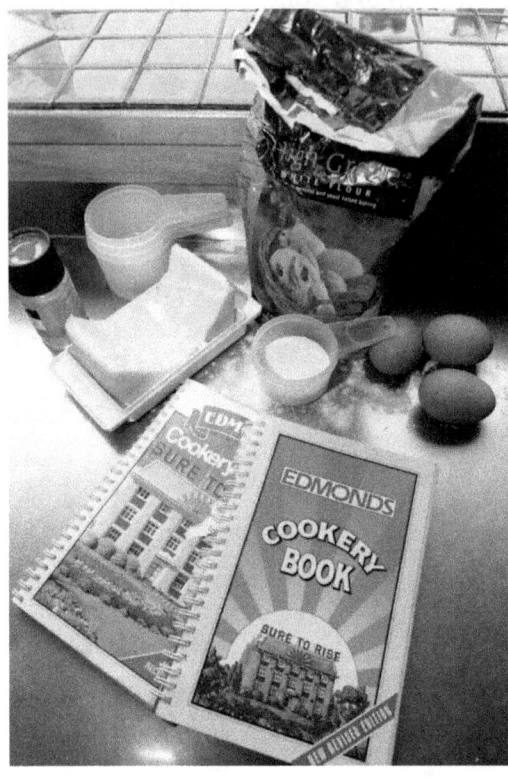

Flicking through the history of Ilott Advertising is like watching black and white footage of New Zealand's unfolding nationhood.

The book, *Creating Customers - The Story of Ilott Advertising*, not only outlines the business fortunes of the country's second ever ad agency, but pays special attention to the social, political and economic factors that shaped both consumer and commercial behaviour.

With a client list naming Edmonds, Creamoata, Bovril, Dulux, Todd Motors and Watties among many others, it is clear Ilott Advertising took part in forming myriad cultural icons. The agency was established by John Ilott senior in 1892 and passed down to his son and grandson. The last Ilott involved in the company, Jack, finally retired in 1982 and the agency was then bought by Ted Bates International.

Jack Ilott passed away in 1999, but not before compiling a history of the agency, and of the Ilott family. Large parts of both books are devoted to his father Sir John Ilott who was a mainstay for 70 of the company's 90 years.

Reviewing Sir John Ilott's life also highlights two important elements of the makeup of a top leader — first is the sheer energy they put into work, you will see him nick-named The Dynamo, a soubriquet which could equally be applied to other leaders (Sir Peter Leitch comes immediately to mind). But critically, Illot illustrates that this energy was not devoted totally to his work, it was an energy spread throughout wide ranging interests, which created a man with a well rounded outlook on life and this contributed to his ability to take advantage of opportunities as they arose.

Sir John was born John Moody Albert Ilott in the small Hauraki town of Te Aroha in 1884. Jack writes in his family history - *The Ilott Story* - that Sir John remembered being lifted up by his father to see the bright red glowing sky in the wake of the Tarawera eruption in 1886.

He became the managing agent in Wellington for the Auckland Star group, and several daily and weekly papers in the South Island, including the Otago Daily Times. His ad-placing agency soon became a business in its own right, following an industry trend which was spawning advertising agencies worldwide.

He won the nickname "The Dynamo" for the relentless attitude to work which had been drilled into him from an early age. But he also maintained a wide range of interests: from music, art, literature and philosophy to trout fishing, tennis and stamp collecting.

His love of music led to the love of his life. When the Musgrove German Opera Company brought their Wagner repertoire to New Zealand in 1909, the 27-year-old was struck by Australian singer Hazel Hall. They eventually married in Melbourne in 1912 and returned to New Zealand, where Jack was born a year later.

Jack later writes that one of his mother's greatest achievements was being accepted by John Jr's parents who "had strict ideas and to them the stage was an anathema, and all performers were the lowest of the low. [Hazel's] mother-in-law said, at the end of her life, that she couldn't have found a better wife for her son if she had searched the whole world."

The couple's second child, Mary Elizabeth, had spina bifida and died after three months. Suzanne Ilott was born in 1926, eventually married Ian McKellar and moved to England in 1953. Suzanne's daughter Shona McKellar says she knows "The Dynamo" nickname suited her grandfather down to the ground.

"He was a man of tremendous energy and interested in many different things ranging from business, art and music to supporting many charities.

"He was also extremely sociable and made friends all over the world. I think one of the things that I remember most was how international my grandfather was in his outlook, probably far more so than most of his contemporaries in New Zealand."

Sir John was eager to extend the Ilott network and persuade British corporates to trust him with their New Zealand bookings. In 1922 he spent six months on a reconnaissance visit to the United States, Canada, Britain and Europe. But it was another five years before he opened a London contact office, which helped maintain working relationships in an age when letters took a month to travel the high seas.

"He set up offices in London and Australia and wasn't daunted by challenging established British advertising agencies," says Shona McKellar.

Advertising suffered through the depression and war years: paper shortages meant newspapers were whittled down to six pages. Jack Ilott records that income in 1934 was only half of what it was in 1929, but by 1936 some smart investments had the company back into the black.

Sir John also experienced close calls with death - there were at least four occasions where The Dynamo's life could have been cut tragically short, writes Jack. Sir John was "desperately ill" during the influenza epidemic before a doctor's whisky bottle breathed life into him.

Then in 1933 he developed botulism and paralysis from eating infected food while in the United States. The other three who had eaten from the same can died but "John Ilott was a tougher bird", writes Jack.

During the early 1950s Sir John picked up a life-threatening infection after a minor operation but pulled through.

In 1952 the company's 60th anniversary was a time of celebration rather more than it had been 10 years earlier. It was also the year Sir John decided finally to hand over the chief executive post after 35 years. He stayed on as chairman, but had more time for his directorships of outside companies and involvement with charitable and philanthropic organisations.

Sir John was a founding member of the Rotary Club of Wellington in 1921, and as district governor of Rotary New Zealand helped form the New Zealand Crippled Children Society [now CCS Disability Action]. He also served as a director of Rotary International and later as second vice-president of the international movement.

He also chaired the Nuffield Trust until 1971 and the McKenzie Charitable Trust, and he was a trustee of the National Library, the National Art Gallery and the Dominion Museum. He donated his collection of etchings and engravings to the National Art Gallery, now part of Te Papa.

Sir John was knighted in 1954 by the Queen in Wellington for his services to the community.

From 1950 on he served on eight commercial boards, including National Mutual Life Association, McKenzies Department Stores and Golden Bay Cement.

In 1960 he established The John Ilott Charitable Trust which still provides assistance to organisations for the purposes of improving literacy, parenting, sexual education, women re-entering the workforce and advanced training for highly skilled people in the arts and for women's and young children's educational and research projects.

Jack Ilott notes that Sir John was also the first to establish a comprehensive superannuation plan, arrange for long Christmas holidays and initiate optional flexible hours of work.

He remembers his father as "an all-rounder with a great zest for life".

"He was a far-sighted man with natural enthusiasm, energy and drive and worked well with people of all ranks. He was a great innovator, motivator and expansionist and was the key man in the success of the business and its long-term reputation for good service.

Sir John Ilott passed away in 1973 aged 89.

+ Sources for this profile were the books written by John Ilott's son Jack - Creating Customers - The Story of Ilott Advertising and The Ilott Story and an interview by William Mace with Sir John's granddaughter Shona McKellar

Chapter Seven

MISTAKES? I'VE MADE A FEW

In 1982 Sir Stephen Tindall opened a single store in Auckland with initial capital of just $40,000. From those humble beginnings arose The Warehouse, the iconic and supremely successful chain of red sheds now ubiquitous across New Zealand. Now The Warehouse has an annual turnover of more than $1.5 billion. It can even lay claim to being one of the most influential businesses in the country - The Warehouse concept sparked a revolution in the way New Zealanders shop, drove competitive prices, sparked a return to suburban shopping and has seen its staff conditions and culture imitated by other businesses well beyond the retail sector. By anyone's standards, the success Sir Stephen has overseen has been phenomenal.

The perfect person, then, to talk to about failure.

Why? Consider that, through vehicles such as his private company, K1W1 Ltd, he has become virtually a one-man venture capital fund. Sir Stephen estimates he has invested well over $100 million of seed funding and venture capital into a number of start-ups and early-stage businesses, from biotech to high-tech and high-export potential businesses.

It's his own money he's putting on the line: a very personal risk.

And while Sir Stephen has enjoyed success, there's always failure. "In venture capital, which is really what I am doing, you get one or two that are superstars, you get about four or five that are okay - they do quite well but not sensational - then the rest of them are failures which you basically lose money on," he says. "You just have to make sure the good ones make up for the bad ones."

Even more pertinent, because it helped mould his character as a businessman, is to look back at his first foray into business – which ended in failure.

Sir Stephen was 19 and admirably entrepreneurial. He decided to set up a coffee bar at Hauraki Corner, on Auckland's North Shore, a well-

Sir Stephen Tindall

chosen spot with plenty of passing traffic: to prove this, it was the very location where another entrepreneurial success story, Sir Peter 'the Mad Butcher' Leitch, established a highly-successful second store which laid the foundation for the growth of his butchery franchise.

Sir Stephen partnered up, fitted out the coffee bar, opened - and within six months was in such trouble he was forced to sell.

"In those days I used to do a bit of musical comedy, and I met a guy who was quite a few years older than me," he recalls.

"I think we were doing the *The Sound of Music* and he and his wife were at a loose end and were looking for something to do. They said they had some capital, and they wanted a bit more and they wanted a business partner. So I got involved and we bought building materials and fitted out a new business.

"We didn't realise at the time that we had undercapitalised ourselves. The actual cost of fitting this coffee bar out was a lot more than we had anticipated. The budget on the sales wasn't accurate, so we weren't selling enough. And we found quite quickly because the other party wasn't able to actually come up with the capital they said they had, we were in trouble. Where I was lucky was managing to find someone to buy the business off us; we were able to pay all the creditors and get out of jail."

Over-capitalised and unable to sell enough to balance the books: a short sharp lesson in Economics 101.

It's not an unusual tale. Sometimes, such failures seem to be all around us, on a very public and substantial scale, involving even seemingly the most blue-chip of companies.

In 2001, Air New Zealand required a $1 billion government bailout to avoid collapse after a disastrous investment in the Australian airline Ansett, which itself had failed after years of under-investment, poor management and the impact of brutal competition. In 2008, dairy giant Fonterra found itself embroiled in the public relations disaster of being linked to contaminated Chinese milk products, which had caused infant deaths, the collapse of its business partner Sanlu and the resulting loss of that investment.

Think Bridgecorp, think Bluechip. Billions were lost as a plethora of finance companies collapsed during the Global Financial Crisis, both here and overseas. Indeed, two years after the GFC was officially judged to have ended, the International Monetary Fund estimated the cost of bailing out banks, mopping up so-called toxic assets, and providing various capital injections and guarantees came to a staggering US$11.9 trillion - around a fifth of the entire world's annual economic output.

Failure on such a large scale is almost incomprehensible. But beneath those global and big corporate failures which dominate headlines are smaller, more mundane failures.

Roughly 40,000 businesses close down each year in New Zealand. They did last year. They will this year. Nothing to do with international credit crunches, simply the vicissitudes of business.

And perhaps, despite the seemingly never-ending international crises, it is on those mundane failures that we need to concentrate to gain a little perspective - a more philosophical view about the nature of failure, the nature of risk. Nothing ventured, nothing gained.

Sir Stephen Tindall, who takes his place as a figure amongst those bleak statistics, understands then the nature of failure - and its importance in business. Asked if it is good to fail, he is unhesitating. "Absolutely," he says: the painful experience of that coffee bar all those years ago was good for him and has stuck with him ever since.

"It made me realise there were things that we did then, that I have never repeated since," he explains. "So I think failure is important: because you learn."

Dame Wendy Pye is even more forthright: "You have to make mistakes to be successful." She quite rightly aligns success with risk. It is only through risk that you achieve reward, but you cannot avoid the prospect of failure. "I put the dice on the table, on the roulette table and then I roll the roulette and as long as 80 percent of the time you come out okay you stay in business," Dame Wendy says. Perhaps as an owner operator, she has a greater entrepreneurial appetite for risk than many in corporate life. She is instructive on how failure should be managed, advocating an almost brutal self analysis. "You cut your losses, you move on in life and you basically say that's a mistake. What I do with all my mistakes is that I record them, I write them down, I say where I went wrong and I do a lot of thinking. I record them so, therefore, never will I ever make that mistake again. You need to be honest with yourself – not blame other people, not say the economic climate was wrong, because you are the person who made the mistake. No one else, you made the mistake so you should be accountable for that mistake."

In this they echo the sentiments of US management expert Russell Ackoff, introduced in earlier. Ackoff was always an advocate of learning in the real world – he estimated 90 percent of what you need, you learn on the job. And the key for him, just at Dame Wendy expressed, was that you learn from mistakes: "You never learn by doing something right because you already know how to do it. The only opportunity for learning is to identify mistakes and correct them." There, expressed by Ackoff, is the raison d'être for this chapter - sharing some anecdotes from our business greats who share his philosophy that if you fail, make the most of it by learning the painful lessons so you never repeat them.

Tony Falkenstein provides an apt case study. You will recall his words of wisdom from *The Zen of Management* – to take a stepped process in your plans to launch a venture, to set achievable goals in a growth profile that is sustainable and sensible, don't bet it all on the first step. Here's where you learn in more detail how Falkenstein came to this belief through a hard-won life lesson. He would rather no one else had to live through such an experience, because when he encountered the first major failure of his career, he lost almost everything.

"Back in the early 1980s I was with a company, Optical Holdings," he says. "We launched Le Specs sunglasses. It was a very, very successful company. From when I came in the share price was 38 cents, and when I left three years later it was over $12, so I got a lot of media accolades and customers loved me, everything I was doing was turning to gold. I thought I was infallible and I said 'gee, hey it's time I did something myself.'

"I had a [customer] base of pharmacies who really just loved me. For three years I'd given them products, they had all sold through, and they had all made good profits out of it, so I had a great reputation with them. I'd seen in *Fortune* magazine that Swatch Watch was very successful in Europe and the US so I went to Hong Kong and got Swatch look-a-likes and launched them under the brand name Z Watch.

"I rang up the importer here of Swatch watches - and you can always get something out of the receptionists - talked about when they were going to launch, how many colours, how many models, what their pricing was. We matched ourselves against them. They were $69.95, we were $49.95, they had a one-year guarantee, we had a two-year guarantee, they had six designs and three colours, we had 12 designs and six colours.

"We did the distribution in pharmacies and department stores and, again because of reputation, we got a lot of window space. We had a lot of what we call wallpaper – posters, in effect - which were bright red with this big Z in it. We were trying to give the impression of being Swiss without saying it. We launched the same day as Swatch in September and between September and December we sold 27,000 watches and Swatch sold 6000, so it was very successful.

"We didn't realise we had a problem until after Christmas. What happened was those watches got sold for kids for Christmas Day and the plasticiser in the strap got very brittle. So the moment you put the watch on it broke. Instantly. We got about 27,000 watches back. I made about $600,000 from the sale of my shares in Optical Holdings, all that had gone into this company. I lost the lot. And really, lost more because I didn't want to put the company into receivership, because reputation is your most important asset. So I paid out. We got them repaired, or anyone who yelled loud enough we just paid the cash back, which was probably quite a few of them.

"Because I had the two-year guarantee, for two years I was getting calls from pharmacists who were left with watches; consumers, just constantly. And that got to me more than the money. Fortunately, I got right down, but we kept our house and that to me was the most important thing. But I think it was just the constant abuse I got. That was my low point. It was tough."

And yet, Falkenstein stepped back into the fray. He got back into risk – and with life lessons under his belt, made a success, running multiple companies and passing on those lessons to people just starting out.

"You get on with life," he says. "I've made a lot of mistakes. 'Gee I blew that', I probably say that once a month. I really think it's important to realise when you have made a mistake and say 'what I learnt there was …'"

It's clear why Falkenstein urges up-and-coming entrepreneurs to manage risk at a comfortable level so that if the worst happens, they can handle it. Incremental growth isn't timidity: its sensible assessment of risk and shrewd planning. And perhaps Falkenstein simply did not plan well enough in one crucial aspect – but more of that below.

First, it's worth further reflection on Falkenstein's anecdote to concentrate on another key point – reputation. He won his opportunity to get his product into the market because his reputation opened doors and people trusted him. Reputation can bring real practical gains. While it may seem a soft attribute, it has hard, tangible benefits. Again and again, reputation is an issue emphasised by the business leaders we have met, from Sir Stephen Tindall to Dame Wendy Pye to Sir Peter Leitch to Douglas Goodfellow. Call it honesty, integrity, authenticity – it all adds to a reputation in the market which can bring real, measurable benefit. It takes years to build. It can take moments to lose. While Falkenstein struggled to salvage himself from the failure of his venture, losing his fortune, he determined the one thing he would not lose was his reputation. He avoided taking the easy path of bankruptcy and opted instead to brave it out – even putting his home at risk – so that he could pay out his pharmacist retailers, at least maintaining a reputation that he would look after their interests. They would not have been pleased with him for upsetting their customers, but he ameliorated that by at least making sure there was no loss of money for them. And, while he dealt with the crisis, it was largely a personal one. Beyond his immediate retail base, the rest of the market was oblivious to his failure. To all intents and purposes his marketing of Z Watches looked to have been another success. This was not deceit. He managed a disastrous situation with good business skills, putting it right and containing the damage. He did the right thing by all those directly impacted. We all make mistakes. It is how we react and recover which sets us apart. His reputation, deservedly, stayed intact.

There is a marked parallel between the personal experience of failure that each leader reflects on from their careers, the big scary mistake that stopped them in their tracks and made them think, and the single important life lesson that they impart when asked to share their wisdom.

We met media baron Alan Burnet earlier, where he urged communication as his greatest piece of advice. Communication – or lack of it - lies at the heart of what he counts his greatest mistake. His mistake is also a classic example to spend some time considering, because it illustrates an organisational challenge facing many businesses. Burnet was attempting a major structural change to the way his business operated. All too often, just as with Burnet's attempt at structural change, it's a challenge which ends with failure.

"The biggest mistake I made is we had a large number of small companies, some of them were printing give-aways, some of them were printing weekly publications, others were doing commercial printing: a whole host and wide range of printing and publishing. I tried to bring them all together under one complex. I bought quite a big, large complex and I thought we would get a lot of savings, efficiencies, and all those sorts of things under one good general manager."

What Burnet describes is the sort of organisational change critical to the survival of businesses. To ensure long-term success a business must be innovative – that concept of innovation may seem slightly out of place in this discussion. But that is because innovation must not be defined solely as new product creation. Innovation must equally be seen in improvements to production techniques, to means of marketing, and to change in the way a company is structured. Companies must review the way they are set up and make adjustments – be it to lower costs, to promote synergies or simply to redesign the company so that it can be more responsive to the business environment it operates in. Burnet's plan for a merger of multiple small divisions into one centralised management structure, physically housed together, is a transformational structural change which was eminently sensible and logical. It promised cost gains, streamlined processes and improved management. It is also a classic example of the preparatory change needed to set the foundation for scaled growth to a bigger operation.

So where did it go wrong?

Burnet says: "I didn't give it enough thought and people reacted unfavourably to losing what, to some of them, would have been fairly cosy little positions, and they couldn't adapt to the new environment."

Sadly, his experience is all too typical. Change too often encounters resistance from staff. And Burnet could tick off a textbook list of the roadblocks that arose – self-interest, lack of understanding and distrust. Burnet had seen a strategically-sound opportunity and moved to transform his business. Structural change needs to be driven in a top-down approach. But in this case, the change was too strongly driven by Burnet as leader and he had failed to embrace the middle management who would enact his plans. This highlights a key leadership learning – leaders can, and should be, enablers of change to achieve growth. They can also be significant inhibitors, because of the way they go about trying to change the company. Where a leader is too single-minded, perhaps too isolated (and here we have echoes of the discussion in previous chapters about communication) an organisation will fail to change or, where growth was the plan, 'fail to scale'.

Burnet is not alone in making such a stumble. Amongst the business greats, Sir Rod Weir has a similar tale of attempted scaling of an operation at speed. "My biggest mistake was trying to integrate businesses outside the business I knew and understood so well," he says. "The business was not successful and I didn't have the depth of knowledge to fix it."

Such changes need careful planning. Once it is clear an organisational change is needed, then there must be an examination of how best to implement it – which should encompass predicting potential resistance and, critically, diagnosing why such resistance will arise.

Strategies can then be designed to mitigate those issues and allow the change to proceed as smoothly as possible. There are many ways to go about this, one theoretical tool, useful in visually clarifying the issues involved, is 'force field' analysis – a concept pioneered by US psychologist Kurt Zadek Lewin (1890-1947), an expert in the study of group dynamics. The theory is founded on the Newtonian realisation that every change has forces that propel it and forces that resist it: true not just for physical science, but also for organisations. Such analysis provides an elegant way to portray those forces and assess their relative strengths and merits. Often, it reveals that while strategic design represents the official structure of a business, behind it is an unofficial political structure – with political power (defined simply as the ability to get things done, or stop them being done) not always held by those you would assume hold it given their position in the hierarchy. This is closely allied to the underlying culture of a business: it's near impossible to enforce change on a company culture. But cultures can be swayed, can evolve and will react to a leader who can fire enthusiasm and can instill their passion into others.

There are two superb quotes, drawn from a useful book by Christopher Wilt called *Real Leaders Don't Do Powerpoint – How To Speak So People Listen*, which highlight this perfectly. First is from Jerome Solon Felder (1925-1991) who gained fame as a US blues songwriter under the name Doc Pomus. When asked his secret to writing a hit song, this is how he replied:

"Find the shortest distance between your insides and a pencil."

So too with a leader: find the shortest route between the vision in your mind and the hearts and minds of those you lead - your team, the wider company, and even your customers, so all of them can feel the same passion you do.

Antoine de Saint-Exupéry (1900-1944) was a man of many parts, a French aristocrat, a pioneer aviator and the author of the novella, *The Little Prince*. His words on how to communicate are particularly apt to any business leader contemplating structural change: "If you want to build a ship, don't drum up the men to gather the wood, divide the work, and give orders. Instead, teach them to yearn for the vast and endless sea."

Here we see that, inevitably, once the diagnosis and analysis is finished, the success or failure of business change comes down to communication and selling the vision.

Analysis assists in pinpointing the areas of tension, and then, armed with the knowledge of where the objections will arise, the leader needs to address those areas and then sell their vision. Ideally a single, sweeping speech would be enough but in reality you will need to engage in education and where necessary, to negotiate.

Critically, understanding what the objections are and answering them doesn't mean simply acquiescing to what others want. Instead an understanding of the roadblocks - often the genuinely-held fears of otherwise dependable people - allows a smart leader to package their plan in a way which deals with those issues. They have to ensure there is participation by at least those who will be responsible for carrying through the change and that the business will achieve what it needs to.

Burnet rightly identified all of this in his blunt assessment of where he made his mis-steps: "I should have taken that much more quietly and listened more to the people involved because there was an extraordinary range of people - printers, journalists, managers, accountants. That was the biggest mistake I made, and that took a year or two to recover. And that was hard work. The lesson I learnt from that is, consult and talk to your people. You don't always necessarily adopt fully what they say to you - but you learn from it. And in the end you get a balanced judgement. And the people are far more receptive to what you are trying to do. Keep them informed, tell them what you are about, have confidence in them."

People too were the pivot for Sir Richard Carter, for whom mistakes had a personal edge. His greatest mistake: "Trusting some people too much and finding when circumstances changed, so did they."

If you reflect back on the discussion in an earlier chapter about getting the right people on the bus, this wry comment takes on extra resonance. Hiring the wrong person can lead to enormous problems – and so too, can establishing business relations with the wrong partners. And here remember also Dame Wendy Pye's troubled relationship with a distributor for her books overseas. Go back to that Falkenstein anecdote above. Review it again and you will also find a similar problem at its heart – Falkenstein actually almost won his big entrepreneurial venture, he had executed a perfect piece of ambush marketing and outslugged the international Swatch marketing machine. What let him down was his sourcing of product. He chose the wrong supplier and didn't product test sufficiently before going to market.. If his Z Watches had been of better quality, without the catastrophic failings of the brittle wrist band, then the venture would have succeeded.

Instead it failed. Because of one crucial mistake.

Every honest leader admits to making mistakes. And every smart leader says it was one of the best things to happen to them because it taught them lessons they carried throughout their successful careers .So the chief lesson from this section – you will make mistakes. Embrace them for what they give you - life lessons.

Sir Wilson Whineray has a pragmatic word of advice: "Toughen up and face it and don't run away from it."

He follows it with an insightful comment: "And of course the wonderful thing I think about the human being as an animal, it is the one animal that has the fantastic ability to adapt. It has since the dawn of time."

That is profound counsel. You have the ability to transform that failure into a strength if you take it to heart and adapt.

Sir Ron Carter had another useful perspective on failure which was highlighted earlier, but is useful to repeat here: "To be successful over time you have to have brought success to other people and yourself and if society has got a future, it's got to be one that embraces everybody, not just a few winners."

But these men, sadly, are a rarity. Not just because they are among the few who have risen to the top in business, but because of their philosophic acceptance of failure.

Back to Sir Stephen Tindall.

Not all New Zealanders, he says, take failure in their stride. "There is a culture that would say 'gosh, if that person failed we have to be really careful about extending credit or backing that person with capital again,' " he says. "So I don't think we are that accepting of failure. I think we do tend to get pretty dark on failure, pretty quickly."

It is something almost engrained in the New Zealand psyche.

Take rugby. We will at times lose to the Springboks or the Australians. All will be despair. Then we will win. All will be joy. "I think it would be a lot easier on everybody if we accepted failure occasionally, that you can't win all the time. But that you can learn."

He contrasts the New Zealand attitude with that in the USA. "In fact in the US, which you have got to say is probably the most successful country for growing business over the last century, they have had this sort of badge of honour which runs around failure."

If we are truly to grow economically, we may need to adopt a similar attitude. Failure then is not to be frowned on. It is indeed, quite possibly, a key indicator of a leader, says Sir Stephen: "If we take some of New Zealand's greatest leaders, and I think of Peter Blake, who had four failures in his round the world campaign with the Whitbread before he won - that is the true mark of a leader, somebody who can pick themselves up and go at it again."

Just look at Sir Stephen Tindall.

ROY SAVAGE: Pragmatic Change

Where others saw a lone storeman importing and selling industrial gloves out of a small corner in a Wellington warehouse, Roy Savage saw an opportunity.

In 1958 the 24-year-old was working at the Griffin Savage Company, a confectionery-importing company his father, also Roy, had brought to the North Island after World War I. It was then the young man spied the career path he had been waiting for.

Forty years later, his workplace safety clothing and equipment companies, NZ Safety and AlSafe in Australia, employed 400 staff and turned over $130 million a year. It is a business story of personal pragmatism, mergers and acquisitions, government policy, selflessness, and, above all, a reliance on common sense. It is those qualities which built an enduring family business.

His relationship with his father was pivotal in his first days in business. "We were both in the Allen St building when the Hawkeswood [soon to be NZ Safety] company started - we were always working together from the same office, knew what each other was involved in and doing, had lunch or morning tea together and compared notes."

Savage went through Victoria University, studying accountancy under his father's gentle encouragement but learning through experience suited him more than classroom lectures. In this he is reminiscent of Ted Lees. He says his university attendance was largely structured around his rugby commitments; the post-Labour Weekend cram for exams was common. He decries the modern economies of tertiary education that mean students no longer have as much time for extra-curricular activities. After finishing accountancy and travelling extensively, Savage returned to complete a Bachelor of Commerce, play rugby and work with his father at Griffin Savage.

During one boom the company subsumed a food importer that held an agency for an Auckland industrial glove producer under the name N. Hawkeswood Company.

"That's what caught my eye," says Savage. "It fascinated me because at that stage safety was just starting to be pushed by the Labour Department as a good idea. Men were just starting to realise, 'hell, why am I putting up with tearing my hands out handling all these bricks instead of wearing gloves?' The idea of safety clothing in those days to a Kiwi male was thought of as a bit feminine."

Despite the "she'll be right" attitude of tradesmen, New Zealand's import licensing meant it was burgeoning as an industrial nation. Successive governments passed work-safety legislation and equipment standards were established in concert with equipment retailers such as Hawkeswood. Savage set out to give same-day service to the growing market and opened several regional stores, including in Auckland.

He was also honing his negotiation skills and ended up buying his competitor's business. He then made the risky decision to sign a 10-year lease on a warehouse building in Auckland, the rental for which "was about three times the profit we had made in the previous financial year". But an expansive strategic game plan made it necessary. Hawkeswood bought stakes in other equipment distributors and manufacturers, and in 1975 these were all brought together in one entity under the name NZ Safety. Soon after, the company also bought competitors Wormald and James North. They eked out market domination by purchasing existing businesses in towns throughout New Zealand, but keeping them under local management.

"When they sold to us they released their capital, which was then available to buy the bach at the beach or a new car, and they were on a secure salary and were part of the decision-making. All of that helped the momentum to keep going."

It wasn't so clear cut when NZ Safety opened an Australian branch in the early 1980s, though Savage knew it was the right thing to do.

"My view was that any business, to be successful, has to be in both Australia and New Zealand. When you go to overseas principals or when you're trying to become a distributor for an overseas manufacturer, New Zealand is a pretty small pie, and if you can say you're in both, they do start to take notice."

But where 14 warehouses were servicing three million Kiwis, the Aussie operation started with only one warehouse among the three million of Sydney. It was losing money. Savage decided the company needed to "disguise" itself by buying the safety division of an established engineering company, which allowed the company to break even in Australia.

Then "a fair-weather friend" arrived on the scene. "The Bank of New Zealand had started in Australia in a big way and was almost like a government agency trying to help New Zealand businesses expand there. They had tonnes of money to lend and you could almost see them rubbing their hands when you came in to see them, saying, 'Is there any way we can help you?' and 'Oh, is that all you want to borrow?' "

A loan helped NZ Safety buy AlSafe, and a 50 per cent equity deal with an engineering supplies company helped repay the loan in the aftermath of the 1987 sharemarket crash. The company later reacquired that firm's half-share and was in the clear, eventually splitting shareholdings between the management team and then selling both companies to Howard Smith for nearly $80m in 1998.

However, during the 1990s, import deregulation began to affect the family business. The confectionery market was in chaos because the walls had come down, and the market was being flooded by "corner dairy" importers. Disillusioned with the food market, Griffin Savage sold its confectionery business and now imports Crabtree & Evelyn homeware into its own stores, as well as the Smith & Caughey, Ballantynes and Kirkcaldie & Stains department stores.

The business also transformed to have a focuses on investments through private equity subsidiaries - itself a skill he learned from his father. Twenty-five per cent of proceeds from the sale of NZ Safety and AlSafe went into the private equity pot which he and his daughter Catherine Savage - formerly managing director of AMP Capital Investments - have managed jointly since 2007.

It seems fitting for Savage to have his daughter in the company where he learned to wheel and deal under his father's supervision. However, she earned her stripes elsewhere and some might say she's got a few tricks to teach her dad.

"There's a bit rubbing off both ways - Catherine is a broad- picture person and I've always been 'crossing the Ts and dotting the Is', and being careful about the administrative details. I think we've got a good combination going, although I'm a bit too old to learn new tricks."

Catherine says: "What Dad has taught me is there's a few basic principles of business that are really important and a lot of the other stuff is just noise. I think it's actually quite complementary us working together. We've never had an argument, it's been really the most amazingly pleasant experience and I've learnt so much just because it's a different approach, part of which is his natural personality. That's why he gets asked to do a lot of volunteer or governance work - because he's such a thoughtful man."

His analytical expertise and problem-solving nous are certainly in high demand with Wellington's sporting, dramatic and charity organisations. Fostering the Life Education Trust's mission to teach children about health and wellbeing has been a particular passion of Savage and his wife of 51 years, Renate. Its founder, Trevor Grice, mentored one of the couple's sons. He also supports Wellington's young tennis stars, as he "can't stand to see a couple of thousand dollars stand between sportspeople and a world-beating goal". Then there's the Gryphon Theatre and the establishment of the Foundation for Economic Growth with Charles Gilmore and Hugh Templeton in 2004.

"It's this idea of creating something that was worthwhile," Savage says. "I always thought the safety business was something that was for the benefit of society, and if you're doing something that you feel will benefit your fellow man then that helps. The whole idea is if you can look back at the end of your life and say, 'Well, what I did was something of value to people, it gave them a happy and worthwhile life and that I didn't let anyone down'."

+ Sources for this profile were a one to one interview by William Mace with Roy Savage and an interview with his daughter.

TONY FALKENSTEIN: Creativity Unleashed

Of the countless attributes you could assemble to describe the traits of a successful businessman surely laziness would not feature.

But for Tony Falkenstein, one of the country's most acclaimed entrepreneurs, it is a quality he sees in himself and – still more surprisingly – rates as one of the keys to his success.

How can that be for a man who runs three businesses - Just Water International, Bartercard and office furniture company Buro? It's how Falkenstein illustrates there is no single template for an entrepreneur – each is individual and they can come from anywhere.

For instance 'hard working' is a typical epithet for any top businessman. Falkenstein's response: "I'm not, I say I'm lazy."

"If you have to work on a consistent basis more than 50 hours a week you must be doing something wrong. You can't be that important that you have to spend 100 hours a week on your work."

He would rather be relaxing on a beach than in the office. It's that desire to get balance between work, family and sport which has driven the structuring of his businesses so they run at peak efficiency – without needing his constant attention.

Similarly, competitiveness would normally be accounted a hallmark attribute for a business leader. Again Falkenstein says he's not. But he likes the trait in other people. So another key to his success is that he hires the right people with the right skills to compensate for what he lacks.

Which brings us then to what he regards as his single greatest attribute. Adding ideas. Thinking outside the box. Dreaming.

It is the core of entrepreneurial skill and leadership. Perhaps the antithesis of management.

"In business the things I've done have been fairly creative, have been different. The one skill I've got is that I can see things very quickly outside the box."

He says most people get dreaming knocked out of them by school, but he never did. He was an average student at Auckland's Onehunga High School. He passed School Certificate but failed University Entrance on his first attempt, having to re-sit.

However if they had a grade for dreaming he rates himself as an A plus and says that is what ultimately proved important.

"You make more money by using your brains."

This fits within his broader philosophy on business – enjoyment. If you're not in business for profit and fun, then what are you doing here, he says.

"I'm just playing a game."

It's a slice of wisdom gained through a career tempered by highs and lows, involving dancing girls (yes, really, more on that later), Swiss watches, lucky breaks and the new oil of fresh water.

A potted biography then. Falkenstein is the son of hard up German Jewish refugees who had fled the Nazis. In the new land his father, a doctor of law, found it hard to adjust, but his mum who had never worked before hit the ground running, displaying the entrepreneurial flair that rubbed off on her son, eventually becoming a real estate agent. "I never realised we were poor," says Falkenstein. "I just always had a job."

From school he made it to university and gained a commerce degree. His first inroad to corporate life was with Polaroid in the 1970s where thinking outside the square got him noticed. He helped create the concept of photos on the back of credit cards by inventively tackling a way around Muldoon era taxes, an idea which changed the way Polaroid operated in selling "ID" cameras globally. He became the youngest regional general manager in Polaroid and was destined to head overseas to become a global corporate leader.

But he turned his back on that, choosing to stay home and help care for aging parents. His father later developed Alzheimer's. Regret? Not on your life.

He joined Optical Holdings and there showed his eye for a good marketing opportunity – invited to a Chamber of Commerce luncheon and given just 10 minutes to pitch a new sunglasses product, he ushered in four dancing girls donned in Le Specs. And the rest is history for an icon of the 1980s. He was feted as a business leader. "Everything I touched turned to gold."

Then came utter disaster. Lulled into thinking he was infallible he launched his own venture, importing knock-off copies of Swatch watches. The products were inferior, broke, he lost a fortune and almost his house. "It was that tight"

Of this period he simply says "I was very low."

But he got back into business and found himself, in the fall out after the 1987 share market crash, buying an arm of a dismantled business for just $1. Red Eagle Corporation was born and grew into a multimillion-dollar business.

Then came other ventures. His water company, Just Water International, went public in 2004, branding him as one of the country's more successful entrepreneurs.

In New Zealand today with much handwringing around a brittle economy, the tyranny of distance from market and cost of exports is there still opportunity for new entrepreneurs to enjoy the same level of success?

There has never been more opportunity, says Falkenstein. Online has removed the reliance on capital intensive start ups and there is a world of opportunity in service industries.

So what is the key challenge then? Typical of Falkenstein: The biggest challenge, he says, is yourself.

+ *Sources for this profile were a one to one interview by David Gadd with Tony Falkenstein. Tony Falkenstein has contributed much to the chapters in this book, but his is an interesting enough out look and story of success that a further profile was deserved.*

THE GREATEST: Short biographies of all the Business Hall of Fame laureates

More than 100 of the greatest business leaders in the country's history have been inducted as laureates into the Fairfax Media New Zealand Business Hall of Fame since its inception in 1994.

They cover the full panoply of industry sectors, range of talents and stretch from the earliest years of our economic growth to current times. Within their ranks are instantly recognisable names and legendary businesses and brands. But alongside them are also the more obscure, and discovering those leaders, learning something of their background and contribution to our economic history, is a rewarding experience.

They each started their careers within a particular sector but many, typical of the entrepreneurial people they were, expanded into other areas of business and endeavour. You will see common themes emerge – shrewd and opportunistic risk-taking, restless energy, vision, strategic foresight, and humility. Another marked aspect which shows through again and again, an underpinning almost universal in their ranks, is an ethos of giving back and reinvesting some of the wealth they have made back into the community.

The laureates are profiled here in the years in which they were inducted, up to the date of printing this book. For more you can go to this website: http://www.businesshalloffame.co.nz.

1994

Sir Woolf Fisher (1913–1975)
Manufacturing

The first Labour government played a key role in Woolf Fisher's decision to become a whiteware manufacturer.

From 1934 he and Maurice Paykel were content to sell imported fridges and washing machines. But the government's tough import controls, introduced in 1938, persuaded Fisher & Paykel to start manufacturing its own products. This was the start of the partners' success.

Fisher, whose famous saying was "Today's luxuries are tomorrow's necessities", laid the foundations for an iconic New Zealand company.

He played a major role in establishing the Outward Bound course at Anakiwa and set up a charitable foundation to provide travelling scholarships for teachers and principals.

Sir William Goodfellow (1880–1974)
Dairy industry

William Goodfellow was an accidental pioneer in the dairy industry — he gained a foothold in return for a debt owed to his ironmongery — but once established he changed the face of dairying forever.

Through the Waikato Co-operative Dairy Company and later the New Zealand Co-operative Dairy Company, he led the industry to adopt international best practice. This included providing a quality premium on cream, establishing milk grading, introducing the first dairy company laboratory in New Zealand, starting a farm dairy instruction service and promoting group herd-testing.

Goodfellow was also an advocate of international marketing of dairy produce and influenced the government to set up the Dairy Produce Control Board in 1924

Sir Bryan James Todd (1902–1987)
Energy

Bryan Todd's first taste of the oil industry came when his father opened a service station in 1912. A brother established a national car dealership in 1923 and another brother set up a car-assembly plant in 1934.

But Todd's real success came when he entered the petroleum industry in 1929 after being cut off from supplies in a price war. A family company set up in 1933 became Europa Oil — an independent until its acquisition by BP in 1972.

Todd led oil exploration in New Zealand. A joint venture with Shell and BP struck oil at Kapuni, Taranaki, in 1959. A decade later, offshore drilling by the consortium discovered the huge Maui gas/condensate field.

Sir James Fletcher snr (1886–1974)
Construction

Scots-born carpenter James Fletcher became the nation's most important builder. His joinery and house-building business, started in Dunedin in 1908, became the Fletcher Construction Company — the basis of the publicly listed conglomerate, Fletcher Holdings, and a company now part of Fletcher Building.

Fletcher Construction built some of the country's finest public buildings and a number of the nation's first state houses.

During World War II Fletcher took charge of the New Zealand construction industry when the government appointed him commissioner of defence construction, superintendent of military works and controller of shipping. His son, Jim, took over the business that in 1981 became part of Fletcher Challenge.

Sir James Wattie CBE (1902–1974)
Food Production

No greater testimony to James Wattie's contribution to the economy was the acquisition of Wattie Foods by US food giant H J Heinz in 1992. Wattie was not alive to witness the $567 million transaction but the size and shape of the business was a far cry from J Wattie Canneries he formed with Harold Carr in Hastings in 1934.

Wattie expanded the business during World War II, producing dehydrated foods to supply New Zealand and American forces. In 1947 he started quick-freezing vegetables, a process that led to spectacular economic development in Hawke's Bay and Poverty Bay. Wattie's remains one of New Zealand's leading brands.

Sir Jack Newman CBE (1902–1996)
Transport

The Newman name is best associated with stagecoaches and buses yet it was behind the huge forest and fibreboard plant on Nelson's doorstep and an independent airline, Newmans Airways, that became Ansett New Zealand.

Jack Newman, the most important member of the family, joined Newman Bros, in 1920, a business dating from 1879. He became managing director in 1935 and founded Transport (Nelson) Holdings — later renamed TNL Group — in 1938.

Active in the community, Newman also served as president of the New Zealand National Travel Association and was active in the Passenger Transport Federation and the Pacific Area Travel Association.

1995

Sir Kenneth Ben Myers MBE (1907–1998)
Alcohol Industry

Ken Myers was the unsung hero of the liquor industry. He made a reluctant entry into the family business, the Campbell & Ehrenfried Company (C & E), in 1933, sacrificing a promising accountancy career with London-based Whinney Smith & Whinney.

Myers arrived in Auckland in the midst of the Depression and, as C & E's new chairman and managing director, he set about revitalising the liquor company and setting standards for the disorganised and run-down industry. He did this by upgrading hotels and facilities and introducing a rebuilding programme.

C & E's innovations, now taken for granted in the industry, included bulk-beer dispensing systems from tanks, beer gardens, à la carte dining and machine accounting.

Edward Max Friedlander OBE (born 1922)
Retail

Ted Friedlander was chairman and managing director of national clothing retailer Hallenstein Glasson Holdings from the 1970s until his retirement in 1989.

Born in Auckland and educated at John McGlashan College, Dunedin, he joined the Otago branch of Hallenstein Bros in 1939. He rejoined the company after war service and rose through the ranks to join the board in 1954 and become managing director in 1973 and chairman in 1977.

Friedlander served as president of the Otago Retailers' Association from 1963–64 and of the New Zealand Retailers' Federation in 1969. He was also active in the Institute of Management.

Sir Clifford Ulric Plimmer KBE (1905–1988)
Rural Industry

Cliff Plimmer was a great-grandson of Wellington pioneer John Plimmer and continued the family tradition of business success and public service.

He joined stock-and-station agency Wright Stephenson & Company in 1922 as an office boy and worked in most departments before becoming a director in 1945, managing director in 1952 and chairman in 1953.

Plimmer expanded Wright Stephenson into one of the country's largest public companies.

Plimmer was a director of several public companies and a member or chairman of many public bodies including the Taxation Committee (1951), Royal Commission on State Services (1962) and the New Zealand Trade Promotion Council. He was also a trustee of the New Zealand Institute of Economic Research.

Sir William Alfred Stevenson KBE KStJ (1901–1983)
Engineering

Auckland-born Bill Stevenson started work at age 17 in his father's carpentry business. In 1921 the firm bought a Model-T Ford, three wheelbarrows and some picks and shovels and branched out into construction.

Stevenson took over the business after his father fell ill and later brought in his three sons.

During World War II W Stevenson & Sons was awarded several key military contracts and after the war it won major infrastructure contracts.

Bill Stevenson's other achievements were equally impressive. He was a national single and double skulls rowing champion, one of the country's leading sports administrators at international events overseas, an accomplished horsebreeder and a generous donor to good causes.

Sir Robert James Kerridge Chevalier of the Order of Merit (Italy) CStJ (1901–1979)
Entertainment

Robert Kerridge's business career began humbly but before he was 50 he owned and controlled the largest theatre-entertainment organisation in the southern hemisphere.

A consummate dealmaker, he reigned unrivalled in entertainment and cinema distribution.

Kerridge's real success came in the entertainment business when, in 1943, he gained a controlling interest in New Zealand Theatres. In 1946 he entered a partnership with J Arthur Rank Organisation to secure film distribution and by 1947, Kerridge had acquired the Fuller theatres and those of the J C Williamson group, giving him an unrivalled 130-theatre circuit.

Under his direction, the Kerridge Odeon group diversified into tourism, hotels, advertising, catering, publishing, recordings, merchandising, property and finance.

1996

Sir Angus McMillan Tait KNZM OBE (1919–2007)
Telecommunications

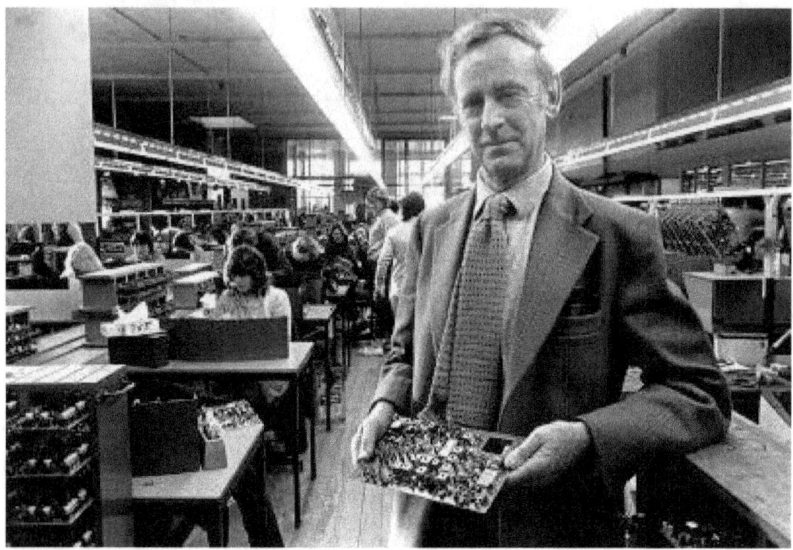

Angus Tait's Christchurch-based Tait Electronics developed an international reputation for radio communication equipment and became a significant exporter.

Tait, whose first job was in an appliance store before joining the Royal Air Force, cut his teeth on the wartime development and maintenance of radar.

Back in New Zealand, he identified a business opportunity when the Post Office introduced mobile radio-telephones for vehicles and in 1951 he built the first Tait mobile phone. The product found a ready market in the ambulance and fire services.

The company went into receivership in 1967 but Tait refused to give up and set up a new company with some of the old staff the following year. He never looked back.

Sir Robertson Huntly Stewart KBE (1913–2007)
Manufacturing

Christchurch-born plastics engineer Robertson Stewart founded Plastics & Diecasting Ltd (the future PDL Industries) in 1944 and was involved in the design, production and manufacture of all products in the formative years.

His strength was his ability to adapt PDL, which expanded into electrical goods and consumer appliances, was a product of industry protection but the business also thrived when the economy was deregulated. Exporting was part of that success story.

Stewart led a trade mission to the Pacific Islands in 1962, was deputy leader on the first trade mission to Southeast Asia in 1964 and led another six trade missions to the region. He also made substantial contributions to the arts and culture in Canterbury.

Sir Jack Richard Butland KBE (1896–1982)
Food Production

Food manufacturer Jack Butland was born in Hokitika but is remembered as a true-blue Aucklander.

He pioneered the processing and packaging of food and the product most associated with him is Chesdale cheese.

But the other side of Butland was his generosity. He was the leading public benefactor of his day, donating at least $500,000 to a variety of causes.

Butland entered the workforce as a bank clerk. Later he worked as a salesman for a rubber company and then decided to go into business, collecting agencies for imported foodstuffs.

He founded J R Butland Pty in 1922, NZ Cheese four years later, Butland Tobacco in 1936 and Butland Industries in 1949.

Chew Chong (1827/44?–1920)
Rural Industry

Guangzhou-born Chew Chong arrived in New Zealand in 1867 and moved to Taranaki. There he identified the jew's ear fungus — "Taranaki wool" — growing on native trees as suitable for food and medicine.

Chew Chong opened a store in New Plymouth and established fungus as a crop, cornering most of the Taranaki trade and exporting it to China. He opened branches in Inglewood and Eltham, trading in a variety of goods including butter which he also started exporting.

Chew Chong opened the Jubilee butter factory in Eltham in 1885, added four creameries and bought the nearby Mangatoki factory.

In 1889 he installed a Hall's refrigerating machine at the Jubilee factory — probably the first freezing machine in a New Zealand butter factory.

Richard William Vincent Izard OBE (born 1934)
Manufacturing

The circular saw-blade company once owned by Richard Izard was one of the country's most successful businesses. Wanganui-born Izard, educated at Wanganui Collegiate School and Massey Agricultural College, returned to the land as a major sheep and cattle breeder after a spectacular foray into manufacturing.

He established Izard Manufacturing Company at Wellsford, north of Auckland, in 1980 with state assistance and during his ownership the company became the largest producer of tungsten carbide-tipped saw-blades in the world, supplying between 30 and 40 per cent of the American home-handyman market. When the company was sold to Irwin International in 1991, it was employing 200 Wellsford people and had a turnover of $50 million.

Sir John Robert McKenzie KBE (1876–1955)
Retail

Melbourne-born fancy-goods store proprietor John McKenzie he came to New Zealand for a holiday in 1909 and decided to set up a chain in New Zealand.

The first McKenzie store opened in Dunedin and the business grew rapidly. It became a public company in 1936 and 50 per cent of John McKenzie's shares were transferred to Rangatira, a private investment company.

By 1980, when the business was taken over, McKenzies (NZ) comprised 75 stores employing 1800 people.

The family name lives on in the J R McKenzie Youth Education Fund, set up in 1938 with a gift of £10,000, and the J R McKenzie Trust, set up in 1940 with £100,000.

Sir Robert Arthur Owens KNZM CBE Order of Merit (Chile) (1921–1999)
Transport

Manchester-born master mariner Bob Owens arrived in New Zealand in 1946 with £140.

He moved to Tauranga where he set up a shipping and stevedoring business (later the Owens Group) in 1953. He was a pioneer exporter of logs to Japan and in 1967 became representative for Mitsui OSK Lines.

Owens became a national figure in 1972, putting together the New Zealand half of the joint venture to acquire the Union Steam Ship Company from P&O.

Owens made his name in local body politics, serving after the 1971 election as mayor of both Tauranga and Mt Maunganui.

In 1982 he led a trade mission to South America and was instrumental in breaking the Australian-led trade ban against Chile.

1997

John Anderson (1820–1897)
Engineering

John Anderson, a Scottish blacksmith who arrived in Canterbury on one of the first four ships, was the father of New Zealand engineering.

His business began in a small blacksmith's shop on the plains at Riccarton "amidst the fern, flax and tussock" and grew to become the huge Canterbury Foundry — the first in the province and a pioneer in making iron lamp posts, screw wool presses, flax-stripping machinery, gas machinery, boilers, dredges and railway bridges.

Anderson was a member of Christchurch's first town board. In 1869 he became the borough's second mayor and was one-time president of the Chamber of Commerce, a member of Lyttelton Harbour Board and chairman of the first licensing committee.

Thomas Russell jnr (1830–1904)
Investment

Irish-born carpenter's son Thomas Russell jnr was articled to an Auckland barrister in 1844, admitted to the bar in 1851 and by age 30 was an acknowledged member of Auckland's commercial elite.

His milestone was helping form New Zealand's capital market, notably with the flotation of the New Zealand Insurance Company in 1859 and the Bank of New Zealand in 1861

By the 1860s he and partner Frederick Whittaker, twice the New Zealand premier, were running the richest law practice in the colony.

A land speculator and goldmining investor, Russell established an intricate network of business and political friendships, not least with Colonial Treasurer Sir Julius Vogel whom he assisted raising government loans in England.

Assid Abraham Corban (1864–1941)
Alcohol Industry

Assid Corban did not start the New Zealand wine industry but he and his family did more to commercialise it than anyone else.

Their West Auckland-based company was sold in 1975 but the Corbans brand lives in premium wines.

Virtually all the developments that led to Corbans Wines' success can be traced to the Corban family and its New Zealand founder.

Born in Lebanon, Assid Corban arrived in New Zealand in 1892, initially working as a trader on the Coromandel Peninsula.

In 1902 he bought a piece of scrubby gumland near Henderson to grow grapes. Seven years later he was selling wine and by the early 1920s his wines were finding favour throughout the country.

Sir (John) Logan Campbell (1817–1912)
Commerce

Logan Campbell, the father of Auckland, earned that title from 1840 when he and business partner William Brown took up residence on Motokorea Island in the Waitemata Harbour until his death nearly 72 years later.

An Edinburgh-born and trained physician, he gave up medicine to speculate in property when Auckland was about to become the capital in 1840 but soon, with Brown, became one of the first Auckland merchants to export directly to England.

His firm became a leading merchant trader and brewer and in 1897 amalgamated with Ehrenfried Bros to become the Campbell & Ehrenfried Company. Campbell's greatest gift was in 1901 when he bequeathed Cornwall Park, Auckland, to the people of New Zealand.

Sir Alfred Hamish Reed CBE (1875–1975)
Publishing

The firm of A H & A W Reed has long since been absorbed by a larger competitor but for many years it was a major player in New Zealand book publishing.

Born in England, A H Reed came to New Zealand with his parents in 1887, worked as a gumdigger in his teens and was later a typewriter salesman (1897) and a bookseller in Dunedin (1907).

His firm ventured into publishing in 1932, specialising in books covering New Zealand, Maori and aboriginal lore, children's tales, education and provincial histories.

Reed began his own writing career in 1935, producing an extensive range of books, many covering his travels as New Zealand's outstanding recreational walker.

James Robert Maddren CBE Chevalier d'Ordre de la Couronne (Belgium) (1920–1998)
Rural Industry

Christchurch-born James Maddren pioneered the exporting and processing of venison and game, sending the first shipments of venison to the US in 1952–53 and later to Europe and Asia.

He was responsible for setting up the first experimental deer farm at Lincoln College, Canterbury, in 1968, to determine the feasibility of farming deer.

He was also a leading light in promoting manufactured exports through manufacturers' groups and trade missions and a prominent company chairman and director.

Maddren's charitable work included the St John Ambulance Association, refurbishment of Canterbury Museum and the businesshouse appeal for a South Island bone-marrow transplant unit.

Sir James Muir Cameron Fletcher (1914–2007)
Construction

Jim Fletcher earned a place in history for building New Zealand's largest and most enduring industrial company.

Born in Dunedin, Fletcher joined South British Insurance Company in 1931 and the Fletcher Construction Company in 1937. He became secretary of Fletcher Holdings in 1940, managing director from 1942–79 and chairman from 1972–81. Under his direction the group expanded rapidly but he saw the need to create a company of international standing which was achieved by merging Fletcher Holdings with Challenge Corporation and Tasman Pulp & Paper in 1981 to form Fletcher Challenge. It was the crowning glory for Fletcher who had played a key role in the creation of Tasman Pulp & Paper.

Sir Francis Henry Renouf Officer's Cross of the Order of Merit (Germany) (1918–1998)
Banking

Wellington-born Frank Renouf was a prisoner-of-war in Germany from 1941–45 and completed his education at the University of Oxford after the war.

He became a sharebroker in 1950, a job that was to be his mainstay for the next 38 years. He established a national share index in 1957, known as the NZUC (later Barclays), and was chairman of New Zealand United

Corporation from 1960–83, Renouf Corporation from 1984–87, Renouf Properties from 1985–88 and Renouf Underwriters Pty from 1980.

Renouf was a casualty of the 1987 sharemarket crash but the losses he and his companies suffered did not undo his sterling contribution to New Zealand.

Sir Thomas Edwin Clark jnr (1916–2005)
Manufacturing

Tom Clark was 14 when he was thrust into the Depression-hit family ceramics business in West Auckland. But the experience at Amalgamated Brick & Pipe was not wasted on him.

He used his impromptu start in the New Lynn pottery to experiment with new products, preparing the company for the opportunity provided by World War II to branch into crockery manufacturing. By war's end a new name, Crown Lynn, was becoming known throughout the country.

Clark and brother Malcolm became joint managing directors in 1964 and the company embarked on a bold set of acquisitions. Clark became sole managing director in 1973 and the following year, Consolidated Brick & Pipe Investments, the parent company, was renamed Ceramco.

Robert Hannah (1846–1930)
Retail

The Hannah name, synonymous with quality and affordable New Zealand shoes, can be traced back to January 21, 1868 when Robert Hanna (originally without the "h") arrived in the Westland gold town of Charleston and took over the footwear business of W G Jackson.

Little remains of Charleston today but R Hannah & Co lives on as a shoe manufacturer and retailer, surviving in a tough consumer market.

Hannah was born near Belfast, Ireland. He sailed to Queensland in 1864 but followed the gold rush to the West Coast. Hannah left the Coast for Wellington in 1874 and founded R Hannah & Co, creating a company with stores nationwide.

1998

Princess Te Kirihaehae Te Puea Herangi CBE (1883–1952)
Maori development

Princess Te Puea, a highly spirited granddaughter of the second Maori king, had barely four years' formal education but, after teenage exuberance, became drawn into Maori politics.

She led Tainui's opposition to conscription during World War I and campaigned after the war to improve her people's living conditions and re-establish Ngaruawahia as the centre of the King Movement. Under her guidance, Turangawaewae was established in 1921.

Despite Te Puea's opposition to the Sim Commission's 1927 offer of compensation for confiscated lands, she maintained good relations with politicians of the day. Her legacy is the national status for the King Movement and the rebirth of Maori crafts, not least waka-building.

Sir Henry Joseph Kelliher KStJ (1896–1991)
Alcohol Industry

Henry Kelliher had already been a Gallipoli veteran, hotel owner, Scotch whisky importer and women's magazine publisher and editor before, at age 34, entering the brewing industry. This was by way of a partnership with the Coutts family who in 1929 had opened the Waitemata Brewery in Otahuhu, Auckland.

Despite the Depression, the brewery was a success and in October 1930 it became a public company, Dominion Breweries.

Under Kelliher's leadership, the company became a major hotel owner and liquor distributor, challenging the industry's major player, New Zealand Breweries. It survives today as DB Breweries, owned since 2004 by Asia Pacific Breweries.

Graeme James Marsh CBE (born 1933)
Manufacturing

Graeme Marsh's contribution to manufacturing was finally recognised officially in 1995 when he was awarded the CBE. It was a fitting tribute to a skilled manager and talented company director.

Educated in Dunedin, Marsh's career developed from chartered accountancy to corporate management. His interests spanned from owning General Motors dealerships, engineering and technology companies to control of rope and twine manufacturer Donaghys where he was managing director from 1988–97.

Marsh served as president of the Otago branch of the New Zealand Society of Accountants, dominion president of the Motor Trade Association, and a member of the Australia and New Zealand Business Council and the Prime Minister's Enterprise Council.

Raymond Watson Hurley (1923–1978)
Manufacturing

Ray Hurley's interest in sailing led him to a naval career in England and New Zealand. Bur it was in business after World War II where he made his mark.

With his parents' money and encouragement, he and brother Desmond (who had a background in the clothing industry) started a corsetry business but they soon specialised in underwear because of a shortage brought about by wartime controls.

From their first factory in Auckland in 1946 they established lingerie-maker Bendon that grew large enough to acquire its main competitor, Berlie NZ, in 1970.

Hurley's died of motor neuron disease in 1978 but his vision for Bendon lived on.

Maurice Paykel CBE (1914–2002)
Manufacturing

Between 1934 and 1938, Maurice Paykel and Woolf Fisher sold imported fridges and washing machines. But import controls imposed by the Savage Labour government encouraged local manufacturing and Fisher & Paykel started making its own machines.

The business remained with the Fisher and Paykel families for 45 years until it was floated in 1979.

Paykel was joint managing director from 1963–75 and chairman and managing director after Fisher's death in 1975. He also had other directorships and was chairman of the Sir Woolf Fisher Trust, member of the New Zealand Inventions Development Authority, member and chairman of the Medical Research Council and active in the Laura Fergusson Trust.

Sir (Thomas) Harcourt Clarke Caughey KBE CStJ (1911–1993)
Retail

Harcourt Caughey was an old-world figure committed to hard work and public service.

He joined the family's Auckland department store, Smith & Caughey, in 1930 and worked there for 63 years until his death — 30 of them as managing director and chairman.

An All Black from 1932–37, Caughey was best known for his service to Auckland Hospital Board where he was a member for 25 years and chairman for 15.

Caughey was also active in the Medical Research Council, the Auckland Medical Research Foundation and the University of Auckland School of Medicine.

He was knighted in 1972 for his contribution to health administration.

1999

John Jones (1808/09?–1869)
Rural Industry and Shipping

Sydneysider Johnny Jones saved sufficient money from working on sealing and whaling ships and as a waterman ferrying people across Sydney Harbour to acquire interests in three whaling ships by 1830.

Starting with a whaling station at Preservation Inlet, Southland, he gained control of the South Island whaling industry.

In 1838 Jones bought a whaling station at Waikouaiti Bay, Otago, and established settlements at Matanaka on the northern end of the bay. As whaling declined, he moved to farming, introducing sheep, cattle and horses, and providing food to Dunedin settlers after the town was founded in 1848. Jones also formed the Harbour Steam Navigation

Company, which became the Union Steam Ship Company.

Sir Ronald Ramsay Trotter (born 1927)
Rural Industry

Born in Hawera and educated in Wanganui, Victoria University College and Lincoln College, Ron Trotter started work as a stock clerk in 1949. He was destined to become a leader in the stock-and-station industry.

Trotter rose to become managing director and chairman of Wright Stephenson & Company, later managing director and chairman of Challenge Corporation, later still chief executive and chairman of Fletcher Challenge and, finally, chairman of Wrightson.

Trotter also chaired or directed a number of outside companies and professional associations. He was the founder and inaugural chairman of the New Zealand Business Roundtable and led the Economic Summit Conference sponsored by the incoming Labour government in 1984.

Sir Laurence Houghton Stevens CBE (1920–2006)
Manufacturing

Laurie Stevens joined Auckland Knitting Mills in 1946, became secretary in 1948, manager in 1952 and managing director from 1954 until his retirement in 1980.

He became a leading figure in the New Zealand textile industry and manufacturing.

Stevens served as president of the Apparel and Textile Federation of New Zealand and two terms as president of the New Zealand Manufacturers' Federation. During the latter term, 1981–83, he played a leading role in negotiations with Australia over the Closer Economic Relations treaty.

He was also a professional company director, serving on or chairing the boards of a variety of companies including a major involvement with Auckland International Airport.

Sir Apirana Turupa Ngata (1874–1950)
Maori development

Born at Te Araroa, East Cape, and educated at Te Aute College and Canterbury College, Apirana Ngata rose to become a talented politician and scholar.

The first Maori to graduate from a New Zealand university college and one of the first of any race to gain a BA and LLB, he was admitted as a barrister and solicitor in 1897 but was more interested in politics, culminating in his election to Parliament in 1905 where he remained for another 38 years.

Ngata held the native affairs portfolio in three administrations, devoting himself to Maori resettlement on the land and to research into Maori tribal history.

Rodolph Lysaght Wigley (1881–1946)
Tourism

South Canterbury sheepfarmer's son Rodolph Wigley co-founded a transport company in 1904, specialising in traction-engine haulage and contract harvesting.

His early interest in tourism and cars led him to import Darracq service cars — the start of the Mount Cook Motor Service.

The business collapsed in 1907 but in 1912 Wigley took over the assets and restarted operations as the Mount Cook Motor Company, which acquired the lease of The Hermitage, Mt Cook, redeveloping the hotel and environs.

Wigley transformed the motor company, which by 1930 was the largest tourism operator in the country. It became the Mount Cook Group in 1976 and is now part of Air New Zealand.

Robert Graham (1820–1885)
Tourism

Scots-born Robert Graham went into partnership with his brother, David, as a general merchant in Kororareka and Auckland in 1842. As a result of developing good relations with local Maori, the Grahams were able to evacuate their stock from Kororareka without loss at the start of the Northern War. In 1845 Robert Graham bought land, including hot springs, on the foreshore of Waiwera, north of Auckland, in the start of a long career of tourism investment and promotion.

His negotiation skills and ability to speak fluent Maori helped him years later gain tourist interests in Rotorua and Wairakei.

Graham's Terrace Hotel at Te Wairoa was destroyed in the Tarawera eruption in 1886.

Nathaniel William Levin (1818–1903)
Rural Industry

London-born Nathaniel Levin arrived in Port Nicholson (Wellington) in 1841 where he set up a drapery, hosiery and haberdashery business known as Levin & Co.

In 1843 he opened a food, liquor, whale oil and whalebone business and also bought a shore whaling station at Cloudy Bay at the top of the South Island.

Levin & Co became a prominent shipping and land agency, general merchant and stock-and-station agency.

Levin was a founding member of the Wellington Club in 1841 and highly respected in the business community. He was appointed to the Legislative Council in 1869, the first Jew to become a member of the upper house.

Donald George McLaren ONZM (born 1933)
Biomedical

Don McLaren, owner of Auckland-based animal remedies company Bomac Laboratories, made the headlines when Bomac made a significant donation to Massey University's Institute of Veterinary, Animal and Biomedical Sciences.

Bomac became the Massey institute's corporate partner — a relationship that went far beyond mere sponsorship.

McLaren's community service was demonstrated in other areas. A keen racing man, he was president of the Auckland Racing Club which he helped restore to profit by good management and sale of surplus club land. He also served on a number of community and professional organisations including the New Zealand Thoroughbred Breeders' Association and the New Zealand Racing Conference.

2000

Francis John Carter (1869–1949)
Manufacturing

Francis Carter's timber career began modestly in about 1895 when he and J W Lee and Arthur Wright opened a sawmill near Levin, processing kahikatea swamp timber.

After clearing the Koputaroa forest, Carter and Wright concentrated on a sash and door factory they had opened in 1897 at Mangaweka, then the northern railhead of the main trunk line.

Carter set up a flaxmill with R W Smith near Taupo in about 1900 but the venture failed and with Wright he re-entered sawmilling in 1902.

Carter's timber interests expanded throughout the North Island, establishing the basis for the large group that became Carter Consolidated in 1951.

Robert Holt (1832/33?–1909)
Manufacturing

Robert Holt arrived in New Zealand in 1859, reputedly with half a crown in his pocket only.

By 1868 he owned a freehold section in Napier and in 1869 he was in business on his own account. He moved premises in 1872, installing a steam-powered sawmill in Hastings St, Napier, and in 1880 a second steam sawmill in Port Ahuriri.

Holt sold kauri imported from Auckland as well as rimu, totara and kahikatea, processing the timber for flooring, posts, palings and house blocks.

By about 1910 the business was trading as Robert Holt & Sons. In 1971 it merged with timbermiller Carter Consolidated to form Carter Holt Holdings.

Alexander Harvey (1841–1919)
Manufacturing

The Mt Tarawera eruption on June 10, 1886 covered Scots-born Alexander Harvey's Te Puke farm with ash, forcing him to abandon it and move to Auckland.

In Auckland he rented a corrugated iron shed in Durham Lane and went into business with his three sons making tin cans. They branched into heavier containers, mainly for the dairy industry — cans, buckets, churns and separators.

Alex Harvey & Sons expanded over the next century into New Zealand's largest diversified manufacturing group, becoming a major corporation in 1969 when it merged with the New Zealand interests of Australian Consolidated Industries (ACI).

In 1985 Alex Harvey Industries was acquired by Carter Holt Holdings, creating a major diversified group.

Sir James Lawrence Hay OBE (1888–1971)
Retail

Otago-born James Hay had an inauspicious start to his career: he left school at 13 to work in a drapery to help support his widowed mother who was bringing up nine children.

In 1909 Hay joined Christchurch department store J Ballantyne & Company, cementing his love for retailing, and in 1929 he joined with others to form his own store, Hay's.

After a successful public flotation in 1934, Hay's grew to become a leading South Island department-store chain, known by its slogan "the friendly store". It merged with Wright Stephenson & Co in 1968 to form Haywrights.

Hay set up the J L Hay Charitable Trust in 1959 and was a Christchurch city councillor.

Edward Elworthy (1836–1899)
Rural Industry

According to Victorian tradition, Edward Elworthy as the third son of an upper middle-class English family was destined for the Anglican Church. But that was not to his liking. Instead he headed for Australia in 1860 where he developed a highly successful farm before putting root down in South Canterbury four years later.

Elworthy proved an excellent farmer, taming the limestone country at Holme Station, 24km southwest of Timaru, and running sheep and growing grain on the same property.

Holme Station became a leading grain-growing run in the colony but Elworthy always looked further afield and was a founding director of the South Canterbury Refrigerating Company, a pioneer frozen-meat processor.

Amy Maria Hellaby (1864–1955)
Rural Industry and Retail

The untimely deaths of Amy Hellaby's brother-in-law and sister-in-law in 1900 and husband in 1902 left her the head of two families and in charge of a large meat company.

She succeeded on her own, expanding Auckland-based R & W Hellaby, supervising the completion of the family mansion and caring for a large extended family.

During World War I she moved to London to be near her sons and nephews serving on the Western Front and afterwards directed the company until younger family members came through.

She was also responsible for the opening of R & W Hellaby's Shortland works at Otahuhu in 1910.

Robert Alexander Crookston Laidlaw (1885–1971)
Retail

Scots-born Christian fundamentalist Robert Laidlaw launched a mail-order business, Laidlaw Leeds, in Auckland, in 1929, along the lines of the US mail-order companies Montgomery Ward and Sears Roebuck.

It boomed with the growth in dairying and the expansion of the railways, dealing wholesale with the farming community only.

Laidlaw Leeds merged with its main rival, the Auckland-based co-operative, the Farmers' Union Trading Company, in 1918, laying the foundation for the country's largest department-store operator, known after 1926 as the Farmers' Trading Company.

The business' success owed much to Laidlaw's entrepreneurship and ability to persuade the directors in 1919 to introduce credit selling and go retail.

Sir Clifford George Skeggs OStJ QSM (born 1931)
Fishing

Southland-born Cliff Skeggs started a fishing business in 1953, creating the largest private inshore fleet in New Zealand. He was a pioneer private investor in deepwater fishing and extended his interests into the transport industry, serving as chairman of Pacifica Shipping, which operated its own airline, Pacifica Air.

But to many, he was better known for his involvement in local politics. He was a member of the Otago Harbour Board from 1965–77 (chairman from 1973–77), a Dunedin city councillor from 1971–77 and mayor from 1977–89. He assisted the community in a number of ways, not least his backing of the Skeggs Foundation to promote sporting endeavour.

2001

(George) Peter Shirtcliffe CMG (born 1931)
Business management

Peter Shirtcliffe might have gone through life as a sharebroker had not fate intervened with the takeover of A S Paterson & Company in 1976.

Shirtcliffe became executive chairman by virtue of a family shareholding and was later managing director of Goodman Group, which the company became in 1979.

He retired in 1986, taking on several directorships including chairmanship of the New Zealand Market Development Board, Telecom Corporation of New Zealand and the New Zealand Trade Development Board.

In 1993 he founded the Campaign for Better Government Trust, which opposed the proposed MMP voting system.

Shirtcliffe also chaired the Enterprise Education Foundation, which merged with the Enterprise New Zealand Trust, founder the New Zealand Business Hall of Fame.

Sir Geoffrey Newland Roberts CBE AFC LM(US) (1906–1995)
Transport

Geoffrey Roberts, knighted in 1973 for services to aviation, is regarded as the father of Air New Zealand.

Born at Inglewood, Taranaki, he joined the Royal Air Force in 1928, serving in England and India before rejoining civilian life in 1934.

In 1946 Roberts was appointed general manager of Tasman Empire Airways (Teal), holding the post until 1958. His term was marked by strong leadership and a vision for developing a national airline.

In 1958 he joined the board of Teal (Air New Zealand from 1965), becoming deputy chairman in 1961 and chairman in 1965. a post he held until his retirement. He was also a director of the National Airways Corporation.

John Brownlow Horrocks CBE MC ED (1920–2003)
Transport

John Horrocks made his early mark on the battlefields of Europe. Aged just 24, he won the Military Cross near Casale, Italy, while serving as a captain with the Royal New Zealand Artillery.

After the war he became commanding officer of the 9th Coast Regiment and served as aide-de-camp to Governor-General Sir Willoughby Norrie.

Horrocks soon established his talent as a lawyer, serving as a partner with Rudd Garland & Horrocks and succeeding practices for 40 years.

His forte was transport and he is remembered especially for his work on the repatriation of the Union Steam Ship Company from P&O to New Zealand and Australian interests in 1972.

(John) Heaton Barker (1867–1947)
Retail

When Heaton Barker, a former cash register salesman, formed the Auckland Master Grocers' Buying Group in 1922 he probably had little idea he was helping create a $4 billion-plus organisation.

His group, later called Foodstuffs (Auckland), helped independent grocers battle price-cutting from farmers' co-operatives and new grocery chains such as Self Help. Two years later the group decided to market its products under the Four Square label. This extended to a Wellington buyers' co-operative in 1930 which later adopted the Foodstuffs name.

Barker ran Foodstuffs (Auckland) from 1922–34 and was a director from

1934 until his death in 1947. He also launched an industry magazine, *Grocers' Review*, in 1936.

Brian Hall Picot CMG (born 1921)
Retail

Brian Picot is remembered by many as an education reformer. But he made his mark in business as joint managing director supermarket operator Progressive Enterprises.

That business was established in 1958 when Tom Ah Chee, Norman Kent and John Brown opened a supermarket at Otahuhu, South Auckland.

Picot became a partner and joint managing director in 1961, introducing family capital and expertise.

Picot retired as a director in 1986 after the company was taken over by Rainbow Corporation but he then chaired the government-appointed Taskforce to Review Education Administration whose *Tomorrow's Schools* report led to the biggest shake-up in the running of schools for more than a century.

Henry Alexander Horrocks (1893–1942)
Manufacturing

Auckland solicitor Harry Horrocks was asked in 1925 for help to develop the 18,321ha Pukahunui Block on the Kaingaroa Plains.

A plan to turn it into farmland had failed and Horrocks formed a company to acquire the block for forestry.

The new company, eventually known as the Whakatane Board Mills, started planting the land and financed the deal by selling forestry bonds to the public.

A former meatworks at Whakatane was acquired as the site for a proposed pulp-and-paper mill. But a lack of capital and import restrictions meant it was July 1939 before an imported board machine was in commercial production.

Horrocks died of pneumonia before the mill proved its worth.

2002

Dr Donald Thomas Brash (born 1940)
Banking

Don Brash completed 14 years as New Zealand's top and most successful central banker before entering politics.

Brash was an economist of international standing, sought after by economists, commentators and journalists during New Zealand's second wave of economic reform in the mid-1990s. He never once mixed monetary policy with politics and, like in his previous jobs, he maintained courteous relations with staff and the public.

Born in Wanganui and educated at schools in Wanganui and Christchurch, and at the University of Canterbury and the Australian National University, he held a number of important jobs in the private sector before his appointment to the Reserve Bank of New Zealand in 1988.

Thomas Henry Ah Chee (1928–2000)
Retail

Tom Ah Chee was a natural greengrocer and shopkeeper, following a tradition established by his grandfather who arrived in New Zealand in the late 1860s.

Ah Chee was born in Remuera, Auckland, but travelled with his parents to Canton, China, in 1931, returning to Auckland as an 11-year-old.

Ah Chee was a bright pupil but his university education was cut short by his father's death and he took over the family fruit shop. It was there he foresaw that large supermarkets would determine the future of food distribution in New Zealand.

In 1958 his vision became a reality with the opening of the country's first major standalone supermarket, Foodtown, at Otahuhu.

Romeo Alessandro Bragato (1858–1913)
Alcohol Industry

An honours graduate of the Regia Scuola di Viticoltura ed Enologia in Conegliano, Italy, Romeo Bragato came to New Zealand in 1895 on secondment from the government of Victoria to look at the possibilities of viticulture and winemaking in the colony.

Touring the colony over several months, he furnished the New Zealand government with a report identifying Central Otago, Canterbury, Nelson, Wairarapa, Hawke's Bay and Auckland as potential major grape-growing regions.

Bragato's greatest contribution was his knowledge on phylloxera, the vine disease that first appeared in New Zealand in the 1880s.

He was appointed New Zealand government viticulturist and oenologist in 1902 with a specific brief to eliminate phylloxera.

Sir Richard Henry Alwyn Carter (1935 - 2011)
Rural Industry

The third generation of a family sawmilling and forestry dynasty, accountant Richard Carter was responsible for creating in 1985 what was then New Zealand's fourth-largest public company.

Carter Holt Harvey, the merger of forester Carter Holt Holdings and manufacturer Alex Harvey Industries, became a group of international standing under Sir Richard's farsighted executive chairmanship.

The merger, which the down-to-earth Sir Richard executed with his twin brother Ken, was one of several major deals that helped internationalise the group.

Under Sir Richard's father, Alwyn, the former family company, Carter

Consolidated, acquired Hawke's Bay timber merchant Robert Holt & Sons, having earlier successfully negotiated rights to mill the Kaingaroa State Forest in the Central North Island.

Sir Timothy William Wallis (born 1938)
Transport and Rural Industry

When Tim Wallis was knighted in 1994 his response to friends and colleagues was "call me Tim".

This accident-prone aviator, a pioneer in deer recovery and founder of Warbirds Over Wanaka, never let success go to his head.

He showed remarkable personal strength at low points in his life, notably in 1968 when he was nearly bankrupted and immobilised in hospital with a broken back after an air crash.

In January 1996 he suffered his fifth air accident, nearly killing himself flying a restored Spitfire aircraft. His response was to praise the St John organisation when he turned the first sod in the construction of a $1.4 million St John ambulance station in Queenstown.

Peter Hanbury Masfen (born 1941)
Investment

Peter Masfen will be remembered as one of the wine industry's leading and most successful investors.

His long relationship with Montana Group (NZ) changed in 2001 when the company was taken over by UK liquor giant Allied Domecq after a protracted battle for control with brewer Lion Nathan.

A New Zealand representative rower in his early life and an accountant by profession, Masfen worked for the Auckland firm of Porter Wigglesworth & Grayburn, becoming a partner.

He consolidated various businesses, land and investments in Collingwood Holdings, which became part of Corporate Investments (CIL). The company eventually changed its name to Montana to reflect its most-prized asset.

2003

(Arthur) Douglas Myers CBE (born 1938)
Alcohol Industry

Douglas Myers was probably New Zealand's most spectacular businessman of the 20th century, turning Lion Breweries into the largest transTasman brewer and a world-class company.

Born to money, Myers turned his head start in life to an unassailable lead, becoming the richest and most successful business leader following his takeover of Lion in 1981.

Under his direction, Lion merged with L D Nathan & Company in 1988 and expanded heavily into Australia. He sold his shareholding to Japanese brewer Kirin in 1998 and stepped down as chairman in 2001.

A passionate proponent of free-market reform, he chaired the New Zealand Business Roundtable from 1990–97.

Major Francis Holmes Chevalier of the Crown of Savoy (Italy) (1874–1947)
Energy

The son of a civil engineer, Frank Holmes had an ordinary South Island upbringing but established an extraordinary career.

He entered the mining industry in South Africa in 1894 and expanded his career to include stints in Australia, Singapore, Mexico, Russia, Nigeria and Uruguay. During World War I he was with the Royal Naval Division, with the rank of major, and served with distinction.

After a period in Abyssinia he moved to the Persian Gulf where, on behalf of the Eastern & General Syndicate, he negotiated an oil concession with the Saudi ruler, Ibn Saud, in direct competition to the British-dominated Anglo-Persian Oil Co. He extracted similar concessions from the rulers of Bahrain and Kuwait.

Sir Wilson James Whineray KNZM OBE (1935-2012)
Business management

Wilson Whineray made his initial contribution to New Zealand through sport when, as All Black captain from 1958–65, he led the national team through a golden age of rugby. But he would also play a key role in business leadership.

Whineray joined Alex Harvey Industries in 1969. It merged with Carter Holt Holdings in 1985 and he became deputy managing director of Carter Holt Harvey, retiring as chairman and a director in 2003.

Whineray was also a director of outside companies and a tireless worker for charity and sports administration.

He was awarded the OBE in 1961, selected as Sportsman of the Year for 1965 and knighted in 1998.

Sir John Packard Goulter DCNZM (born 1941)
Transport

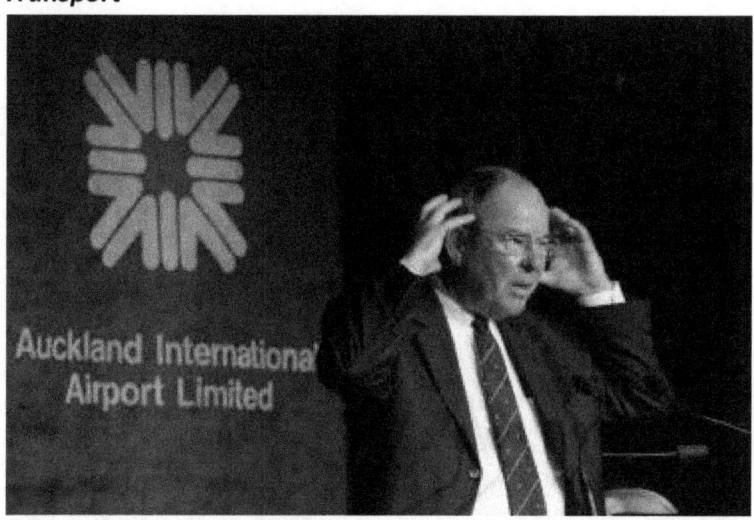

John Goulter had already made his mark in corporate life when, in 1988, he was appointed chief executive of Auckland International Airport.

His achievement was to turn a tired and inefficient airport into a world-class institution with a wide range of attractions and facilities.

He guided the airport through its listing on the Stock Exchange after the government sold its majority stake in the entity in 1998.

As managing director of the new company, he developed airport land profitably and created a user-friendly mini-city. New facilities included McDonald's and a 24-hour-a-day supermarket.

He also turned around staff culture from that of processing passengers to offering first-class, friendly service.

Peter Barr (1861–1951)
Accountancy

Peter Barr's contribution to national business was to establish accountancy as a profession.

His career started when he joined R H Leary's Dunedin accounting and auctioneering business. He became junior partner in 1886 and principal after Leary's death in 1895.

Under Barr's direction the firm became a leading provider of professional services, developing into the national practice, Barr Burgess & Stewart.

Barr retired in 1934, having established himself as the father of accountancy by virtue of being a founding member of the Incorporated Institute of Accountants in New Zealand, its inaugural president and first president of its successor, the New Zealand Society of Accountants. Through his efforts, professional, university-standard education became mandatory for accountants.

Robert Forsyth Barr QSM (1907–1967)
Investment

Robert Forsyth Barr, or Peter Barr as he was better known, was the son of the founder of New Zealand accountancy, Peter Barr. But his education at Otago Boys' High School and the University of Otago, studying accountancy at the latter while working at his father's firm, came second to his love of sport.

He failed his final examination and went on tour to Europe. On returning in 1935 he shocked his family by announcing plans to become a sharebroker. The following year Forsyth Barr was born. Today the firm is a national broking house, reflecting Barr's entrepreneurial vision.

Barr served as Dunedin city councillor from 1944 to 1956 and a director of several public companies.

2004

Eion Sinclair Edgar CNZM (born 1945)
Investment

Dunedin sharebroker Eion Edgar might have moved to Queenstown but his influence continues to be felt in his former home town.

In 2004 he launched his latest project, Queenstown Resort College, a private educational venture in which he is a major shareholder.

Edgar retired in 2003 as chancellor of the University of Otago but maintained his business links to Dunedin through chairmanship of national sharebroking firm Forsyth Barr. He is also a former chairman of the New Zealand Stock Exchange.

Edgar's main interest after business and education is sport. He was president of the New Zealand Olympic Committee and the lead donor of Dunedin's Edgar Sports Centre.

Sir Peter Herbert Elworthy (1935–2004)
Rural Industry

When Peter Elworthy died suddenly in 2004, tributes ranged across the spectrum of the community.

The South Canterbury farming and business leader had always had a high public profile, from his days in the deer farming industry to his national leadership of Federated Farmers of New Zealand during the 1980s.

Elworthy's business interests were equally strong, from his role in the founding of the Ravensdown fertiliser co-operative to being a director of Auckland's Sky City casino. He also championed business sustainability and opposed genetic engineering.

Elworthy's many directorships included the Reserve Bank of New Zealand and the New Zealand Rural Trust.

Sir (Charles) William Feilden Hamilton OBE (1899–1978)
Manufacturing

Timaru-born jet boat inventor William Hamilton left a legacy of innovation and excellence.

His dream of creating a boat that would travel up swift-flowing rivers in the South Island became a reality in 1953 when he developed jet propulsion using water. His first units were marketed commercially in 1957 and later modified to meet international demand in the 1960s.

A self-taught engineer and farmer, he moved into the earthmoving equipment business toward the end of World War II and later perfected the waterjet engine, which revolutionised the world of boat propulsion. He was knighted in 1974 for his "valuable services to manufacturing".

William Murray Gallagher CNZM MBE (born 1941)
Manufacturing

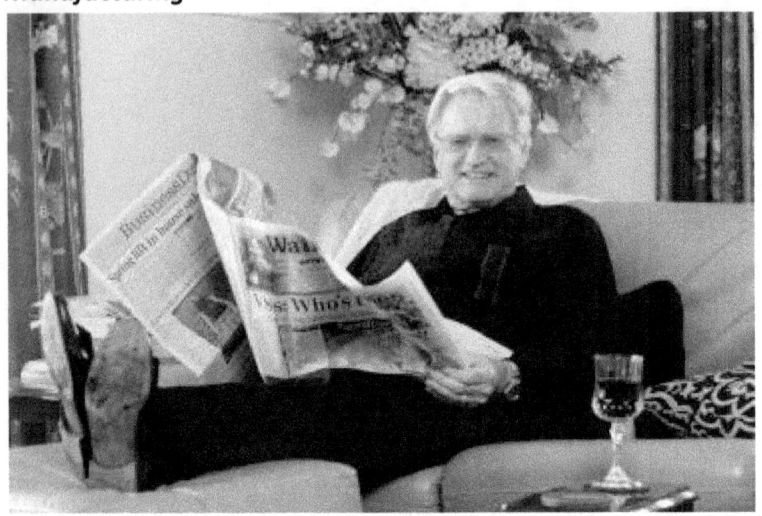

Hamilton entrepreneur Bill Gallagher, a natural leader with excellent communications skills, built a family-owned electric-fence business into a world beater.

Gallagher Group branched into security fences, fuel pumps, plastic moulding and swipe cards. In 2003 it linked up with US Security International as a way to get its security system Cardex into the United States market, worth an estimated $1.2 billion a year

Bill Gallagher won the Ernst & Young Entrepreneur of the Year Award in 2003, adding to a trophy cabinet of honours for his business success.

Gallagher's skills made him a favourite guest for seminars and training sessions in New Zealand and overseas.

Dame Wendy Edith Pye MBE (born 1943)
Publishing

Wendy Pye became a publishing phenomenon when she launched Sunshine Books in 1985. She started the business after a dispute with Brierley Invesments, the new owner of Shortland Publications which she managed. Dame Wendy never looked back, becoming one of the world's largest producers of children's literacy material. Her multimedia titles, including books, television and the internet, sold worldwide.

Dame Wendy pioneered the use of multimedia — animated internet and CD-Rom — to complement the print and other components of her products.

She was a leader in the development of an early literacy programme and learning technologies, and worked with many institutes and universities worldwide to develop strategies for literacy through research.

Howard James Paterson (1953–2003)
Biotechnology

When Dunedin businessman Howard Paterson died suddenly in Fiji in 2003, he left a large gap in the Otago business community.

His vision, energy and determination created a number of successful businesses and underpinned major research and development.

He was the driving-force behind a biotechnology industry based on research at the University of Otago. He also had extensive property and tourism interests and had embarked on plans for a major viticultural development in the Waitaki Valley shortly before his death.

Although Paterson tried to avoid publicity, he received several accolades during his lifetime, including the *National Business Review* New Zealander of the Year award for 2001.

2005

Sir James Nimmo Crawford Doig (1913–1984)
Manufacturing

Glaswegian merchant navy officer Jim Doig launched his business career in 1947 with the formation of United Box Company (later United Empire Box) to manufacture cartons and boxes.

The company expanded rapidly in the post-war industrial era. At its peak in the 1970s and early 1980s, UEB Industries employed 3300 people. It moved into carpets with the purchase of Bremworth in 1967, establishing spinning and scouring plants around the country and exporting products to some 40 countries.

Doig was a leading advocate of union with Australia in the days before CER. He was also the inaugural chairmanship of the Child Health Research Foundation, which was launched in 1971 by Rotary International.

Sir Patrick Ledger Goodman PCNZM CBE (born 1929)
Food Production

Pat Goodman turned his family business in Motueka into a major transTasman food company that still carries the Goodman name.

He became founding chairman of Quality Bakers New Zealand, which merged with Fielder Gillespie Davis and Allied Mills of Australia and Wattie Industries to become Goodman Fielder Wattie in 1987.

Goodman was appointed a special trade ambassador for New Zealand in 1990 and was on the New Zealand Trade Development Board and the Kiwifruit Marketing Board. He had a long association with Massey University and was a member of its Agriculture Research Foundation and patron of its Food Foundation.

Goodman formed the New Zealand Business and Parliament Trust and also supported the arts.

(Harold) William Richardson (1940–2005)
Transport

Southlander Bill Richardson's sudden death in 2005 left a gaping hole in the region's business community. He was governing director of the family-owned holding company, H W Richardson Group, a diverse empire employing more than 1000 staff and turning over about $400 million a year.

The group's 26 companies operated from more than 70 locations throughout New Zealand.

The Richardson empire started in 1878 in the small Southland township of Wyndham with roots in the building industry. Its activities expanded to include ready-mix concrete, transport, fuel distribution, roading, sand, gravel and lime. Allied Concrete, Southern Transport, SouthRoads and Allied Petroleum featured among its better-known brands.

Sir Gilbert Simpson (born 1948)
Software

Gil Simpson's skills as a computer programmer took him to Saudi Arabia in 1976 where he started work on his own ideas about how programmes could be written.

After two years he came back to New Zealand and started developing the Linc product, which was sold to Burroughs (later Unisys) in 1982. He founded Aoraki Corporation, later Jade, which has also become internationally successful.

Simpson has been a director of the Reserve Bank of New Zealand, a member of the New Zealand Business Roundtable and president of the Royal Society of New Zealand. Although once refused a University of Canterbury library card because he was not a graduate, he received an honorary doctorate in science in 2002.

Sir Stephen Robert Tindall DCNZM (born 1951)
Retail

Sir Stephen had retailing in the blood. He worked 12 years for Auckland retailer George Court & Son, a company founded by his great-grandfather, before opening his first discount store, The Warehouse, in 1982.

The business boomed with the lifting of tariffs on imported goods. It was floated on the New Zealand Stock Exchange in 1994 and became the country's most successful retailer.

Sir Stephen was managing director until 2001 and again from 2003 to 2004. He used part of the wealth he created to establish the Tindall Foundation, a charity set up to improve family and community life and foster enterprise.

Sir Harvey Turner CBE (1889–1983)
Rural Industry

Born above his father's Auckland fruit shop, Harvey Turner started work at the age of 12 and became the driving force behind the family business for most of last century.

In 1920 E Turner & Sons combined with a fruit growers' co-operative to form Turners & Growers, which became the country's leading produce wholesaler.

It also gave Harvey Turner a vehicle to modernise the horticultural industry. He pioneered refrigerated produce for export, the exporting of onions and strawberries, and with his sons renamed the Chinese gooseberry the kiwifruit.

Harvey became the inaugural chairman of Fruit Distributors, which took over fruit importing from the government in 1951. The Turner group also diversified into vehicle auctions, importing and assembly.

2006

William Soltau Davidson (1846–1924)
Rural Industry

Well-heeled Scottish Canadian William Davidson arrived in New Zealand in 1865 to work as a shepherd on the Levels Estate, South Canterbury. He rose to become superintendent of 1.2 million ha of farmland for the New Zealand & Australian Land Company.

By 1880 Davidson was exploring meat-preserving, dairying and the potential of refrigerated transport. He also encouraged sheep-breeding and cheesemaking.

In 1882 he saw off the first shipment of frozen meat from New Zealand — from Port Chalmers to London — and was in London when the shipment arrived, having organised the shipping, distribution and insurance. He continued to work for the Land Company until his death, playing a key role in the burgeoning frozen-meat industry.

Keith Wilson Hay CBE (1917–1997)
Construction

Keith Hay started a caravan-building business in Auckland in 1938. He turned to home renovation and the relocation of derelict buildings, a business that thrived after World War II.

He built his first transportable house in 1949 and soon after formed Keith Hay Homes, which pioneered the use of pine in pre-fabricated low-cost houses.

The company, based in Mt Roskill, Auckland, spread throughout the country, and by 2006 had built some 20,000 houses.

Hay was active in the community and the Presbyterian Church as well as being a generous benefactor. From 1953–74, he was mayor of Mt Roskill, and was elected four times to the Auckland Regional Council.

Richard Hudson (1841–1903)
Food Production

A one-time cabin boy who learned to bake, Richard Hudson moved to Dunedin in 1873 where he launched a biscuit, cake and confectionery business. He was probably the first New Zealand trader to sell a pie and a cup of coffee for sixpence. By the 1880s, he was one of the city's most prosperous citizens. Using imported technology, he expanded his business from biscuits into chocolate, making Hudson's a household name. Hudson was an advocate of the eight-hour working day and the first Dunedin manufacturer to ban work on Saturday afternoons. In 1930 the company merged with British chocolate maker Cadbury's to become Cadbury Fry Hudson. Today, as Cadbury Confectionery, it continues to lead its industry.

Richard Michael Hill CNZM (born 1938)
Jewellery retailing

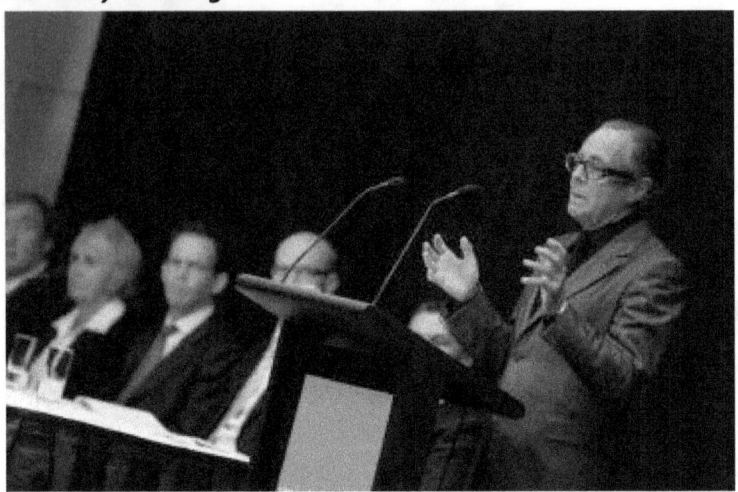

When fire claimed his family home in 1979, Whangarei jeweller Michael Hill's life changed forever. He opened his first shop in opposition to his uncle, for whom he worked.

Within eight years his selling techniques had spread far and wide. When his company listed on the New Zealand Stock Exchange in 1987, it had 10 stores, including one in Brisbane. By 2007 the Michael Hill Jeweller chain had 192 stores in Australia, New Zealand and Canada.

Hill's passion for the violin led to the creation the annual Michael Hill World Violin Competition, a major event for emerging violists.

In 2007 he sponsored the New Zealand golf open at his private course on his Queenstown property.

David Raymond Levene (born 1929)
Retail

David Levene joined his father and uncle's paint business in 1947, taking over the management in 1952 after his uncle's death. He was aged 23 and the business had one outlet. By 1994, when Levene & Co was sold to Skellerup Group, it had 50 stores, paint and wallpaper factories and a total turnover of $150 million. Three years later, after an unsuccessful management buyout, it was placed in receivership. But the name and the business were later revived by a former franchisee.

Levene involved himself in property development and horticulture but found time to help the community. He supported North Shore Hospice, was a patron of Outward Bound and created a charitable trust to assist worthy organisations.

Neville Jordan CNZM (born 1943)
Manufacturing

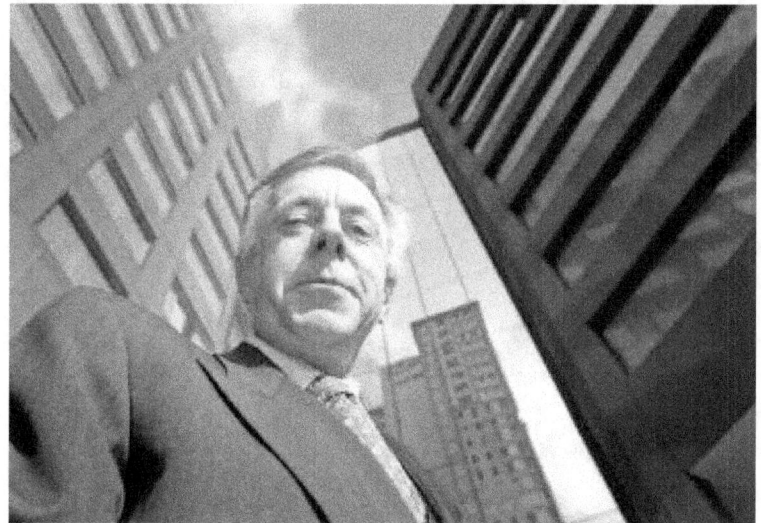

After completing an engineering degree at the University of Canterbury, Neville Jordan worked in civil aviation and for IBM, and spent several years in Europe. In 1975 he founded Lower Hutt-based MAS Technology, a telecommunications microwave company that grew to employ 250 staff and earn more than $100 million a year through exports to 60 countries. In 1997 it listed on the Nasdaq national market in the United States.

In 1997 Jordan received the Governor-General's Supreme Award for Exporting and was later made a companion of the New Zealand Order of Merit. He was inducted into the New Zealand Hi-Tech Hall of Fame in 2004 and in 2006 appointed president of the Royal Society of New Zealand.

2007

William Gregg (1836–1901)
Manufacturing

Irish-born William Gregg establised a coffee- and spice-manufacturing business in Dunedin in 1862. His Gregg's Club Coffee became a national institution, winning medals at exhibitions throughout Australasia.

Gregg was bankrupted in 1894 but rebuilt the business, laying the foundations of a prosperous merchant house.

By the 1960s Gregg's was controlled by the Baker family of Dunedin. In 1984 it merged with Cerebos, a subsidiary of UK-based Ranks Hovis McDougall.

Cerebos Gregg's later came under the control of Cerebos Pacific, a Singapore-based company, and Ranks sold its interests to Japanese company Suntory in 1990.

Cerebos Gregg's bought the local operations of Robert Harris Tea & Coffee Company and sauce and pickle maker F Whitlock & Sons.

Sir Neil Isaac QSO (1915–1987)
Construction

Timaru-born Neil Isaac worked in construction before volunteering for the New Zealand Army during World War II. He and wife Diana, whom he married in Delhi, spent a short time building irrigation dams as contractors in remote areas of India.

After settling in New Zealand, the Isaacs established the Isaac Construction Company and bought a property in Harewood, Christchurch.

The Isaacs progressively bought adjoining land which they replanted to create a much-improved environment and an ideal habitat for native birds.

The Isaac Wildlife Trust, formed in 1977, ensured this environment, now known as Peacock Springs Wildlife Park and the Diana Isaac Conservation Trust, would be retained for the public to enjoy.

Johannes La Grow snr (born 1913)
Construction

Jo La Grouw and John van Loghem arrived in New Zealand from their native Holland in 1951 to sell prefabricated steel-framed homes on behalf of a Dutch company. But they soon realised the vast timber resources offered unlimited potential for natural wood houses that today carry the Lockwood name.

Based in Rotorua, their business developed a unique house construction system that revolutionised the building industry. By the 1980s, Lockwood was one of the country's biggest home providers. It also exported widely, including to Australia and the Middle East.

Van Loghem was bought out in 1989, giving the family 100 per cent control of the business.

Leonard Aloysius Patrick Malaghan (1906–1967)
Manufacturing

Len Malaghan demonstrated an entrepreneurial spirit early on and by the age of 20 he was a qualified manager of a dairy factory.

He developed his own formula for ice cream and in 1935 he and wife Ann opened a milk bar in Wellington — the first in New Zealand to specialise exclusively in ice cream and milk shakes.

Their brand, Tip Top, took off and by 1938 the business was manufacturing in Wellington and Auckland. It came together in 1960 as General Foods Corporation (NZ). Today, Tip Top is a key brand of Fonterra Co-operative Group.

Malaghan was diagnosed with cancer at age 56, leading him to become a major benefactor of medical research.

Neal Hutton Plowman (born 1938)
Service Industry

The Plowmans' laundry and towel-supply service business was started by George Plowman in 1910. It later became NZ Towel Supply & Laundry and was expanded in partnerships with local laundries by George's eldest son, Jack.

Neal Plowman, a third-generation family member, returned to New

Zealand in 1961 from the US and set about expanding the business.

In 1969 it was listed on the New Zealand Stock Exchange to finance diversification into industrial uniforms, cleaning and hygiene services.

Renamed Endeavour Services Corporation, the company expanded its textile rental services throughout Australasian as well as diversifying into other industries.

In 1986 Plowman privatised the company and in 1998 the business was sold to the American Steiner Group.

Trevor Donald Scott MNZM (born 1941)
Business leadership/biotechnology

Trevor Scott became an accountancy partner after graduating from the University of Otago and in 1988 he formed his own advisory firm, T D Scott.

He was one of several businesspeople who regenerated Dunedin's enterprises in the 1980s and 1990s. He was involved in publishing, manufacturing and hospitality and invested in Central Otago's emerging wine industry.

Scott's business connections were put to good use at his alma mater, leading to the commercialisation of Otago's leadership in medical research and biotechnology.

He was diagnosed with cancer and donated $1 million to the T D Scott Professorial Chair in Urology, leading to the formation of a trust that is raising millions more for research and teaching in the area of urology.

2008

Anthony Edwin Falkenstein ONZM (born1947)
Entrepreneurship

Tony Falkenstein was an average student at Auckland's Onehunga High School. He passed School Certificate but failed University Entrance twice and started work as a pastry cook.

More than 40 years later Falkenstein, the son of hard-up German-Jewish refugees who had fled the Nazis, is the toast of entrepreneurs and the hero of his old school.

His company, Red Eagle Corporation, grew into a multimillion-dollar business. His water company, Just Water International, went public in 2004. But Falkenstein was barely known to the wider public until 2003 when Red Eagle underwrote $300,000 to establish Onehunga High as the country's first business secondary school – a role model for enterprise education nationwide.

Sir George Fenwick (1847 1929)
Publishing

Born in Sunderland, England, George Fenwick came with his family to Australia as a child and then to Otago in 1856.

He began work at the age of 12 as a printer's apprentice, the start of a lifelong career in newspapers.

Fenwick gained control of the Otago Daily Times and the Otago Witness in 1877 and co-founded the New Zealand Press Association the following year.

He campaigned throughout his career against social ills as varied as animal cruelty and sweated labour and was a leader and/or promoter of a number of worthy organisations including the SPCA, Patents' and Prisoners' Aid Society, Shipwreck Relief Society, YMCA, Native Bird Protection Society, Hocken Library, Dunedin Diocesan Trust Board and Dunedin Art Gallery.

Sir Roderick Bignell Weir (born 1927)
Rural Industry

Rod Weir started work with New Zealand Loan & Mercantile Agency Company in 1943 as an office junior in the Wanganui office. He was aged 15.

He progressed to the livestock department, and branch livestock managership at Otaki, beginning his long involvement with Horowhenua.

In the early 1960s Weir was moved to the Wellington head office and in 1963, a few months after the merger of Dalgety & Company with New Zealand Loan & Mercantile Agency Company, he resigned to go out on his own as a stock-and-station agent in Levin – the start of a career that would see him establish the Crown Consolidated group and later Dalgety Crown which he merged with Wrightson NMA in 1986.

Ronald Alexander Jarden (1929 1977)
Investment

Lower Hutt-born Ron Jarden, best known as a dynamic All Black wing three-quarter, was a man of extraordinary talent who was successful in a variety of spheres.

Jarden's representative rugby career started when he was 19 when he played on the wing for Wellington. Two years later he was in the All Blacks, having established himself as a rugby genius.

At the age of 26 Jarden quit the game after a short but spectacular career of 37 matches for the All Blacks, including 16 tests. He then devoted himself to business, eventually forming his own sharebroking firm, R A Jarden & Company (later Jarden & Company), which groomed many of the country's finest brokers.

Alan Burnet (born 1921)
Publishing

Alan Burnet can thank Rupert Murdoch for his spectacular career in newspaper publishing and management. It was Murdoch who, having acquired a stake in the Wellington Publishing Company, was responsible for Burnet's appointment as general manager in 1964.

Burnet, an accountant, had been general manager of his home-town newspaper, the Wanganui Chronicle. His move to Wellington would ultimately change the course of the New Zealand newspaper industry.

Burnet moved quickly to protect the Dominion against possible takeovers by a series of skilful mergers and acquisitions that formed the basis of what would become the giant Independent Newspapers group (INL).

INL's assets were acquired in 2003 by Australia's John Fairfax Holdings for nearly $1.2 billion.

Shariffe Coory (1866 1950)
Commerce

Shariffe Lettoof was the daughter of peasant farmers from Bsharri in the Lebanon Mountains. She married Anthony Coory and in the mid-1880s, with their infant daughter Amelia, the couple sought their fortunes in Australia.

About 1892 the Coorys moved to Dunedin where they joined a close-knit Lebanese community – mostly hawkers – in Walker Street.

The Coorys opened a fancy-goods store before moving into importing. Shariffe, the driving-force in the business, also set up a workshop where Lebanese women made shirts and aprons for the hawkers to sell.

The Coorys' generosity to their fellow migrants taxed their resources but this did not stop Shariffe providing clean and affordable dwellings for bachelor tenants.

Hugh Earle Perrett (born 1939)
Retail

Wellington-born Hugh Perrett has the grocery business in his blood – his father, Harry, was general manager of Foodstuffs (Wellington) from 1937 to 1953 – but Hugh started his professional life in a public accountancy in 1957.

In 1964 Perrett joined Lever Bros (New Zealand) where he rose to national sales controller for Levers and its sister company, Birds Eye Foods (NZ). In 1977 he was appointed general manager of Foodstuffs (Auckland) and in 1979 was promoted to managing director. He became managing director of Foodstuffs (New Zealand) in 1985.

Perrett led the group through a period of spectacular growth and development, expanding national turnover from $1.1 billion to $4.8 billion.

Joseph Edward Nathan (1835 1912)
Rural Industry

The eighth of 10 children of poor Jewish parents from the East End of London, Joseph Nathan had little formal education but was to become a leading player in the New Zealand dairy industry.

By 1873 he was principal of Wellington-based merchant house Joseph Nathan & Company.

From 1901 to −1903 Nathan and his sons negotiated the rights to manufacture dried milk in New Zealand and from 1906 his factory at Bunnythorpe was manufacturing dried milk as well as cheese and other dairy products.

With the growing use of the powder as an infant food, the Nathans changed the name of their product from Defiance Dried Milk to Glaxo, a business now part of the giant pharmaceutical group, GlaxoSmithKline.

2009

Edward Lees - Knight of Civil Merit (Spain) (born 1923)
Manufacturing

If Ted Lees had followed his parent's advice he would have become an accountant but his love of motor vehicles set him on an entirely different course.

Lees joined the Territorial Army in 1939. He qualified as a transport instructor, volunteered for overseas service and was selected the special company service the predecessor of today's SAS.

Lees saw active service in North Africa and Italy from 1942-1945 where his experience servicing and repairing tanks, bulldozers and trucks provided him with an unequalled apprenticeship in heavy equipment.

He returned to the family business in Papakura and moved into heavy-equipment manufacturing and assembly. In 1960 he formed Lees Industries, which produced agricultural and defence equipment, frontend loaders, forklifts, straddle trucks, container carriers and marine engines.

Dr Roderick Sheldon Deane (born1941)
Business leadership

No business leader has served the public and private sectors in New Zealand with more distinction than Roderick Deane.

He joined the Reserve Bank where he rose to be chief economist, head of the economic department and deputy governor.

Deane was able to straddle the sometimes competing worlds of private business and the public sector while holding his own in academia.

He is credited with shifting the focus of economics away from Keynesian-style intervention and state planning toward a greater reliance on markets and stable monetary and fiscal policy.

He enjoyed a stellar career outside the Reserve Bank that included chairing the State Services Commission and serving as chief executive of the Electricity Corporation, chief executive and managing director of Telecom.

Marianne Caughey Smith Preston – MBE (1851 1938)
Retail

Marianne Caughey started a drapery shop in Auckland in 1880. It flourished and her husband, William Smith, joined the business in 1881 and Marianne's brother, Andrew Caughey, joined them the following year.

The growth of the business over the next 30 years owed much to the efforts of all three family members. Smith died in 1912 and Marianne was appointed a director of Smith & Caughey in 1916.

Marianne was a staunch Christian and gave to a variety of religious, welfare and educational causes. Her generosity was recognised in 1935 when she was honoured with the MBE.

She bequeathed her shareholding in Smith & Caughey to the Marianne Caughey Smith-Preston Memorial Rest Homes Trust Board for residential care of the elderly.

George Samuel Beca - CBE DFC (1921 2001)
Engineering

George Beca was just 18 when he joined the Royal New Zealand Air Force in 1939. It was the start of an audacious military career, overshadowed only by his subsequent career in engineering consultancy.

He returned to New Zealand a war hero but instead concentrated on becoming a test pilot. He enrolled in an engineering degree at Auckland University College where his professor recognised his managerial talent and recommended he become a civil engineer.

Beca joined the Gray & Watts engineering practice in 1952 and two years later was made a partner. By the time he retired in 1986, Beca Group was employing more than 500 people in several countries.

He received an honorary doctorate in engineering from Auckland University in 2000 for changing the face of the engineering profession.

Sir Ronald Powell Carter – KNZM (born 1935)
Engineering

When Ron Carter graduated from Auckland University College in 1958 with a master's degree in civil engineering he could hardly have envisaged the spectacular success of his future career.

He joined Gray Watts & Beca in 1959 and over the next 41 years played a key role in developing the group into one of Australasia's most successful engineering consultancies.

Sir Ron worked well with managing director George Beca, who expanded the firm by opening offices in Australia and Papua New Guinea in the 1960s, and Sir Ron followed suit in the 1970s, opening offices in Singapore, Indonesia, Malaysia and Brunei.

Sir Ron was knighted in 1998 for services to engineering and business and in 2000 was awarded one of Auckland University's first honorary doctorates in engineering.

John Plimmer (1812 1905)
Construction and investment

John Plimmer came to Port Nicholson in 1841 and initially earned money cutting timber and burning charcoal and lime until the 1848 earthquake discouraged building in brick.

In 1850 he acquired the wreck of the Inconstant and had it towed to the foreshore near Lambton Quay where he established a private wharf, office and bonded warehouse known as "Noah's Ark".

Profits from the venture enabled him to invest in the local economy and after the 1855 earthquake he devoted himself to building.

Plimmer was active in politics but business was his driving-force. His lobbying for land reclamation, railways and improved port facilities contributed greatly to Wellington's emergence as an economic centre. His most important investment was the Wellington & Manawatu Railway Company.

2010

Sir Ernest Hyam Davis - Cross of the Chevalier of the Legion of Honour (1872 1962)
Alcohol Industry

The spectacular career of Ernest Davis started modestly enough in his father's liquor business. Hancock & Company, in 1892. By 1910 he was running the company and well on the way to controlling the direction of liquor industry.

He worked with his father and brother to successfully fight the prohibition lobby and in 1923 he helped create New Zealand Breweries, a combine of 10 breweries, to fight nationalisation of the liquor trade.

But Davis had an equal commitment to public and community service, being a member of nearly 100 organisations in his lifetime. He was elected as the mayor of Newmarket, Auckland, in 1909 and became one of the most popular Aucklanders after winning the city mayoralty in 1935 and 1938.

Sir Peter Charles Leitch - KNZM QSM (born 1944)
Retail

Peter Leitch left Wellington Technical College at age 15 to work as a telegram delivery boy and later in Wellington butchers shops before moving to Auckland. His chance to be his own boss came when the landlord of a vacant butcher's shop at Rosella Road, Mangere, took a shine to him and financed him into business. Leitch later moved to a shop in nearby Massey Road, which became the starting-point for a national butchery chain known as The Mad Butcher. Leitch was also an active champion of many causes, including his favourite code, rugby league, and favourite team, the Vodafone Warriors. He also chaired The Mad Butcher and Suburban Newspapers Community Trust, which raised more than $1 million for charities.

Sir (William) Douglas Goodfellow (born 1917)
Rural Industry and Investment

Douglas Goodfellow, a son of dairy entrepreneur Sir William Goodfellow, built on his good start in life to become an astute investor and a spectacular donor.

He inherited great wealth but also the Goodfellows' Presbyterian penchant for altruism and modesty. Once the richest New Zealander, by 1995 he had transferred most of his fortune to charitable trusts.

Goodfellow became a generous donor to the St Kentigern Trust, established in 1949 to facilitate the creation of a Presbyterian boys' college at Pakuranga, Auckland.

He also established and funded a postgraduate chair in general practice at the Auckland Medical School, the Goodfellow Unit offering continuing education to doctors and nurses in primary health care, and the Douglas Goodfellow Scholarship in Engineering.

Sir John Moody Albert Ilott (1884 1973)
Advertising

John Ilott changed the face of advertising, using his fortune to promote the arts, literacy and a range of worthy causes. He took over as chief executive of his father's advertising agency, J. Ilott, in 1917, enhancing the agency's reputation for innovative campaigns for a range of businesses and causes. Under his direction, Ilott Advertising went national and spread to London and Australia. John Ilott, who retired in 1952, had helped form the New Zealand Crippled Children Society in 1934–35. He later donated his extensive collection of etchings and engravings to the National Art Gallery. Another of his legacies was the John Ilott Charitable Trust, set up in 1960 to provide assistance to for a range of special projects.

Roy Savage (born 1934)
Manufacturing

Roy Savage's first proper job was an assistant storeman with Wellington confectionary wholesaler the Griffin Savage Company, a business started by his father and Charlie Griffin in 1920.

In 1958 he gained control of N Hawkeswood, a Lower Hutt-based company which had an industrial glove agency. It caught Savage's interest at a time when there was a growing awareness of the need for personal protection. The renamed company, Hawkeswood Safety, later NZ Safety, was expanded to include a complete range of safety equipment sold through branches New Zealand wide and in Australia as Alsafe Safety. When the business was sold 40 years later it employed about 400 staff and had a turnover approaching $100 million.

Bendix Hallenstein (1835 1905)
Retail

German-born Bendix Hallenstein was the son of a mill owner who made shoddy - woollen yarn from rags with some new wool added. It was an inauspicious start to what would become a stellar business career. Moving to New Zealand in 1863, he opened a store in Invercargill but moved the business to Queenstown in 1864. With sawmiller James Robertson, Hallenstein opened Otago's first inland flour mill in 1867 at Kawarau Falls. Hallenstein succeeded Robertson as mayor of Queenstown in 1869 but in 1873 he moved to Dunedin where he established the New Zealand Clothing Factory, the basis of a business that became the highly successful nationwide chain known as Hallenstein Bros.

2011

Thomas Cawthron (1833-1915)
Shipping - Investment

Thomas Cawthron arrived in Nelson from England in 1849, at the age of 15. The goldfields of Victoria, Australia, then lured him at 18. His success as a contractor of miscellaneous goods for prospectors, rather than digging up a gold nugget, lined his pockets. Investing in shares, local bodies, war loans and mortgages at a relatively young age took him further towards the considerable fortune he amassed during his lifetime.

In the mid 1850s, his father's illness brought him back to Nelson where he began his 25 year-long association with shipping as an agent. Although he retired at 51, Cawthron maintained a close interest in his business affairs and travelled extensively. In 1915 Cawthron bequeathed £231,000 (in modern day terms $30-$40 million) to set up the Cawthron Institute, which he also endowed with an enduring ethos of pro-active and pragmatic science. The institute is now New Zealand's largest independent and not-for-profit research organisation, and is a leader in a range of marine and freshwater scientific research and consulting.

Les Hutchins (1924-2003)
Tourism

Born and raised in Invercargill, Les Hutchins started business life with the Hutchins Furniture Warehouse there but the beauty of his Southern surroundings beckoned. He started his South Island tourism operations modestly in 1954 with an 18km walking track, two old boats, two huts and a dilapidated lodge when he and wife Olive bought the Manapouri-Doubtful Sound Tourist Company. It was just the first of a number of acquisitions - he bought Fiordland Travel and began operating under that name, the Te Anau Glow-worm Caves and the Milford Track lake transport operations.

A few years later he bought the vintage steamship TSS Earnslaw in Queenstown and in 1970 began running cruises on the world renowned Milford Sound after gaining the government's tourism monopoly there. His son Bryan, took over running the company and it was re-branded as Real Journeys in 2002, just a year before Hutchins died.

Hutchins became a founding member of the Save Lake Manapouri campaign, named one of the founding Guardians of the Lakes and held that position for 26 years, also spending 12 years on the New Zealand Conservation Authority. He was a founding patron of the New Zealand National Parks and Conservation Foundation after establishing the Leslie Hutchins Conservation Foundation in 1994 alongside the Olive Hutchins Charitable Trust.

Sir Percy Sargood (1865-1940)
Commerce

Percy Sargood moved to New Zealand in 1891 and served as Christchurch and Dunedin manager of the family warehouse, importers, and manufacturers company. In 1903, he succeeded his father, and partner John Alexander Ewen, serving at the helm of that firm from 1903 until his death in 1940. With more than 250 employees, the firm was one of the first to form a staff provident fund.

He also purchased Wanaka Station in 1912 and pioneered irrigation in the area, planning and developing a dam and turbine device on the Kawarau river, to irrigate the Cromwell Flats for orcharding.

He was a popular, public-spirited, and unostentatious man, giving distinguished service to many organisations, including Rotary and, the Chamber of Commerce. Passionate supporters of the arts, Sir Percy and Lady Sargood donated Logan Park Art Gallery to Dunedin in 1927, as a memorial to their only son, Cedric, killed at Gallipoli in 1915. Following Sir Percy's death, in a characteristic gesture, he gifted the bulk of his estate as a trust fund for the benefit of the arts, youth and education. That is the Sargood Bequest which continues to benefit the community 70 years on.

Brian Perry: (1935-2011)
Engineering

Dr. Brian Perry who suffers from Parkinson's disease, is widely respected for his business acumen and for his generosity to others. Perry's entrepreneurial bent emerged when in his late teens, he set up his own earth-moving company in 1954. Brian Perry had noticed that the Waikato lacked a mobile excavator so he purchased, (with the assistance of a loan from his father,) an ex-army GMC truck and mounted an American-made Quick Way excavator. It was the first mobile excavator in the district and demand was brisk in the developing Hamilton region. He then formed Brian Perry Drainage to diversify into pipe-laying, Perry Wellpoint Dewatering System to keep up with the increased scale of pipeline projects and then Perry Metal Protection and Perry Aggregates.

In the 1980s he worked on the Marsden Point oil refinery project and in a joint venture was the first New Zealand company to solely undertake a major pipeline project, the $20m pipeline to Marsden Point. During this decade the group also bought an established quarry in Ngaruawahia from which Perry Quarries emerged.

Financially successful before he was 30, Perry also set up the Perry Foundation in 1976 which has supported many community initiatives with grants and sponsorships. Its flagship project was the Perrinpark Retirement Village and he took a major role in the development of the Waikato Stadium. In 2005 Hamilton City Council awarded Brian the Freedom of the City – its highest honour – in recognition of his five decades of business and philanthropic contributions to the community.

Sir John Todd CNZM (born 1927)
Energy and Investment

The Todd name is now synonymous with New Zealand business and philanthropy. Sir John is the grandson of Charles, the founder of the Todd company, now the country's largest private company.

He started his career at the age of 18 in the Todd Motors Assembly Plant and worked up through the company, becoming Managing Director in 1968. In 1987, as a result of changes in Government Import Regulations, Todd Motors was sold to Mitsubishi and that year Sir John succeeded his uncle, the late Sir Bryan Todd as Executive Chairman of the Group. When Sir John took over the helm of Todd enterprises, the assets were a holding in the Maui and Kapuni Oil and Gas fields and a portfolio of marketable securities. In the subsequent twenty four years Sir John led the company into many successful ventures in energy exploration, production, generation and distribution; telecommunications; property and media. Todd Energy which had a staff of three people in 1987 is today's only truly integrated energy company and has a payroll of over 400 people. Today The Todd Corporation has four main operations. Todd Energy, Todd Property, Integria Healthcare and ARA, a Marlborough based producer of fine wines and has retained its shareholding in SKY and Crown Castle Australia.

Sir John also chairs the charitable Todd Foundation focusing on funding for children, young people, their families and communities and in 1990 helped establish Philanthropy New Zealand. He is a past President of the Wellington Manufacturers' Association, has been a director on the boards of many high profile companies and in 2001 was made a Distinguished Fellow of the Institute of Directors.

On the arts side, he was a founding trustee of the Arts Foundation of New Zealand and among other organisations, has been a trustee of the Queen Elizabeth II Arts Council and the Royal New Zealand Ballet.

Anne and David Norman (born1945/49)
Retail

Anne and David Norman have worked together for over 35 years. Their first enterprise was a small building development company of which David was the foreman and Anne ran the office. From this humble beginning, their business interests have grown so that today they collectively operate nine brands, over 650 retail outlets and have approximately 10,000 employees in New Zealand and Australia.

Anne Norman was born and raised in Auckland where she attended Epsom Girls' Grammar. David Norman was born in England, immigrating to New Zealand with his family when he was two years old. His family first settled in Mangakino before shifting to Kaitaia and then to Dargaville. When his family moved to Auckland in1962 he attended Kelston Boys' High School.

The pair are active philanthropists with their primary charity being the Leukaemia and Blood Foundation. They chose this charity as both have lost siblings to a leukaemia-related disease. Additionally the University of Auckland's faculty of Medical and Health Sciences offers an annual grant, the Anne and David Norman Fellowship in Leukaemia and Lymphoma Research.

2012

Sir Graeme Douglas (born 1929)
Pharmaceutical

It started with a cough, $500 in capital and a desire for a big challenge. That was the genesis back in 1957 for what has become Douglas Pharmaceuticals with an annual turnover of about $145 million. Sir Graeme Douglas started with one small pharmacy in west Auckland's Te Atatu at a time when New Zealand laws prohibited ownership of more than one shop. For Douglas, manufacturing naturally followed. He started selling his own brand of products. Much of its annual turnover eventually came from exporting to more than 35 countries. In 2011 Douglas Pharmaceuticals produced more than 455 million tablets, 270,000 litres and 31 metric tonnes of pharmaceutical medicines, liquids and creams.

Alfred (Bill) Gallagher (1911-1990)
Agribusiness

Bill Gallagher was an entrepreneurial dairy farmer based in the Waikato. He invented a number of time-saving, cost effective devices, including the Gallagher electric fence which is now used throughout the world. The Gallagher Group which he founded is now globally recognised for its technology in animal management as well as in security systems, fuel systems and contract manufacturing and employs close to 1000 people. Gallagher's son Sir William (Bill) Gallagher Jr, who was inducted into the Hall of Fame in 2004, now runs the multimillion-dollar company which has an annual turnover of $200 million.

Sir Patrick Higgins (born 1938)
Construction

Sir Patrick Higgins is Chairman of Higgins Group Holdings, a leading company specialising in the construction of roads and infrastructure. Based in the Manawatu, Higgins employs over 1200 people throughout the country. Along with his father Dan, and brothers Bernard and Michael, Sir Patrick founded the Higgins Group as a family business.

When his entry to the Hall of Fame was announced Higgins said he saw it as an award for both himself and the company. "All along, I feel I'm just the leader of the group. I happen to be the lucky person, with the assistance of a lot of people, to get the company along." The advice he would give to other business owners was simple, he said. "Do what you know and do it well. Be passionate about your business and don't get overstretched financially and just don't get overstretched at all."

Graeme Lowe (1935-2012)
Agribusiness

Businessman and philanthropist Graeme Lowe was a pioneer of the modern meat industry. During his career he was credited with helping keep New Zealand's meat industry at the forefront of innovation and leading technologies worldwide. Born in Newcastle-upon-Tyne, Lowe arrived in New Zealand when he was 23. In 1964 he bought Dawn Meat in Hastings with two partners and from there grew the Lowe Corporation which he led until his death. Son Any Lowe paid him tribute: "We will remember him for his relentless energy and work ethic, his leadership, innovation, passion and the strong values he instilled in all of us, which included giving back to the communities we work and live in." In his home region of Hawke's Bay, he donated millions of dollars to support the local community.

Thomas Macarthy (1833-1912)
Brewing, investment

Thomas Macarthy established breweries in Charleston and Wellington, and went on to hold a number of offices including director of the Bank of New Zealand. His estate, the T.G. Macarthy Trust, has distributed over $58million.

Mary Jane Milne (1840-1921)
Millinery/Drapery

Mary Jane Milne bought an Auckland millinery and drapery shop in 1867 with her sister Charlotte. She was well known for her energy and ability, and was active in the company, Milne & Choyce, until her retirement in 1908.

2013

Sir John Anderson (born 1945)
Banking

Sir John Anderson started his career working with Deloittes by day and studying accountancy at night. He joined the new formed merchant bank Southpac in 1972 and became Chief Executive in 1979. He led the organisation through mergers with The National Bank in 1989 and ANZ in 2003. He retired as Chief Executive of ANZ National in 2005 and has since served on a number of boards as chair or director. These boards have included agriculture, health, media, industry, property, banking and other community roles, including chairmanship of New Zealand Cricket for 12 years.

Sir George Fistonich (born 1939)
Agribusiness

Sir George Fistonich always had strong ambitions from an early age of becoming a winemaker. He leased two hectares of land from his father when he was just 21 years old and with just an acre of vines, he started making wine commercially under the name Villa Maria. Sir George has been a pioneer of the New Zealand wine industry ever since. Sir George set up a winemaking and viticultural cadet scheme within Villa Maria, and the company was also one of the founding members of Sustainable Winegrowing NZ. Sir George was knighted in 2009 for his services to the wine industry and he received a Lifetime Achievement Award at the International Wine Challenge Awards in London in 2011.

Sir Colin Giltrap (born 1940)
Motoring

Sir Colin Giltrap's passion for cars began at a young age , and he bought and sold Morris Minors cars as a teenager before opening his first car dealership, Monaco Motors, in Hamilton in 1966. Sir Colin's empire extended through the Waikato to Auckland and then across the Tasman and into the United Kingdom. Sir Colin has mentored many young motorsport drivers including Indy driver Scott Dixon, AIGP drivers Matt Halliday and Jonny Reid, and teenage star Mitch Evans. He is a life member of Yachting New Zealand, Patron of the McLaren Trust and a proud supporter of the Starship Foundation and many other recognized charities. Sir Colin was knighted in 2012 for services to motorsport and philanthropy.

Sir Dryden Spring (born 1939)
Agribusiness

Sir Dryden Spring has spent a lifetime at the forefront of New Zealand business, in a wide range of industries, particularly in the agriculture and banking industries. He was chair of the NZ Co-operative Dairy Company from 1982 to 1989, and then chairman of the New Zealand Dairy Board for the following 10 years. Sir Dryden also represented New Zealand's interests in Asia for many years as a member of the APEC Eminent Persons Group which drafted the APEC Vision of "Free and Open Trade in the Asia Pacific", and the APEC Business Advisory Council. He was also a trustee of the Asia NZ Foundation for 10 years and Chairman for five years. Sir Dryden was awarded an honorary Doctor of Science by Massey University in 2000, and knighted in 1994 for services to the dairy industry sector and to New Zealand.

Hugh Green (1932-2012)
Construction, Investment

Hugh Green was born in Ireland and left school at the age of 12 to work with livestock and at cattle fairs. He worked in Scotland, England and Australia before he was 20, and then settled in New Zealand. Hugh and friend Barney McCahill formed a company that grew to become one of the major civil construction firms in the country. Hugh went on to have interests in engineering, construction and property investment. Hugh established the Hugh Green Trust in 1968, which became the Hugh Green Foundation in 1998. The foundation gives away $1.5m to $2m each year and has supported organisations including St Vincent De Paul Society, the Fred Hollows Foundation, Diabetes New Zealand and Medicine Mondiale.

Mary Innes (1852–1941)
Brewing

Mary Jane Innes was born in Wales but immigrated to New Zealand in 1870. After marrying husband Charles, the couple worked together in a brewery. Charles was the brewer and Mary Jane was the business manager. After Charles Innes was declared bankrupt in 1888, Mary Jane took over the management of the Te Awamutu Brewery. A year later she took over Waikato Brewery as well. As a female living in the late 19th century, Mary Jane was never publicly acknowledged as the business owner. But she went on to create a soda and bottling factory, and her forward thinking laid the foundations for Waikato Breweries and also for soft drink giant Oasis Industries – now New Zealand's largest bottling company.

Val Barfoot (1897–1987) & Maurice Thompson (1907–1968)
Real estate

Val Barfoot and Maurice Thompson created a real estate firm that is synonymous with real estate in New Zealand today. Val Barfoot bought a Newmarket land agency business in 1923 and 11 years later Maurice Thompson joined the firm. The business boomed following the end of the Second World War and by 1956 they had 15 branches throughout Auckland. Barfoot & Thompson is now New Zealand's largest privately owned real estate company, and is still run by the Barfoot and Thompson families. The business that Val and Maurice grew now has over 1,400 salespeople in 62 branches throughout Auckland and Northland. Maurice passed away in 1968. Val retired in 1973 after 50 years in the business, and died in 1987.

+ *The majority of these profiles were compiled for Fairfax Media by renowned business journalist and historian Graham Hunt.*

FIND OUT MORE

If you have enjoyed this book, found it useful and want more, you can access further From The Top content:

For more on the Fairfax Media Business Hall of Fame including some videos:

http://www.businesshalloffame.co.nz/

For videos of interviews with specific laureates who contributed to this book, including Sir Stephen Tindall, Sir Wilson Whineray and Dame Wendy Pye:

http://www.youtube.com/user/FromTheTopVideo

To enhance your personal development and understanding of the business environment ensure you keep up to date with the latest in business news by regularly visiting:

http://www.stuff.co.nz/business/

To give us feedback on this work email us at:

fromthetopfeedback@gmail.com

FINAL WORDS

The lives of the laureates of the Fairfax Media Business Hall of Fame encompass enormous success, and moments of abject failure. They show the mix of resilience, luck, intuition, deep thinking and risk taking necessary to shrug off setbacks and capitalize on opportunity. They reveal the key to nearly all successful entrepreneurs has been relentless drive, an ability to think outside the box, values, respect for others and a desire to give back to the community.

But most of all, our laureates show that if you want to get to the top, you need to be dedicated and prepared to put in hard work. That is the real secret to success in business - and to success in every worthwhile venture in any field of human endeavour.

Perhaps their examples will inspire and motivate you to rise to the top in your own chosen field.